Grattan O'Leary

RECOLLECTIONS OF PEOPLE, PRESS, AND POLITICS

FOREWORD BY
ROBERT L. STANFIELD

INTRODUCTION AND PERSONAL POSTSCRIPT BY
I. NORMAN SMITH

MACMILLAN OF CANADA / TORONTO

Canadian Cataloguing in Publication Data

O'Leary, Grattan, 1888–1976.
  Grattan O'Leary : recollections of people, press, and politics

Includes index.
ISBN 0-7705-1523-1

1. O'Leary, Grattan, 1888-1976. 2. Canada—Politics and government—1911-   * 3. Statesmen—Canada—Biography. I. Title.

FC556.O54A3   971.06'0924   C77-001179-9
F1034.O54A3

Printed in Canada for
The Macmillan Company of Canada Limited
70 Bond Street, Toronto M5B 1X3

CONTENTS

LIST OF ILLUSTRATIONS

ACKNOWLEDGEMENTS

A small band of people joined devotedly, in various ways, in persuading and helping Grattan O'Leary to get his story down on paper and then into a book. John Gray, Hugh Kane, and Kenneth McVey for Macmillan, aided by Ivon Owen; Peter Dobell, Thomas Van Dusen, Gordon Fairweather, M.P., Miss Jean Macpherson, Mrs. Vera Bouffard, and Gail Nicholls, his executor. Whatever hand I may have given Grattan with his book was made easier by the encouragement of Moira, his daughter, and Dillon and Maurice, his sons. I hope I have not let him down, nor them.

I. N. S.

The two passages from *The Journal Men: Smith, Ross, and O'Leary of the Ottawa Journal* (Toronto, 1974) are reproduced by permission of the Canadian Publishers, McClelland and Stewart, Limited, Toronto.

FOREWORD

I have some qualifications for writing a foreword to these memoirs of Grattan O'Leary. He was, after all, my landlord at Stornoway and a tenant gains some insight into his landlord's character, especially when that landlord is Irish.

Unfortunately for me I knew Grattan O'Leary only when he had become in years an old man. What an experience it would have been to have known him when he was young in years. I say young in years because he was young in mind and spirit even on his deathbed.

I have not seen these memoirs, but I believe they were prepared near the end of his long life and concern public more than personal matters. Yet I hope they convey something of the quality and the flavour of this man who could fight for a cause with passion and yet listen to and understand another point of view, this man who could criticize you and attack your position vehemently and yet leave you feeling you had been treated with rare courtesy, this man who could be a fierce partisan all his life and yet recognize generously the value of his opponents' works and admire many opponents deeply.

While I respected Grattan O'Leary's intelligence and insight, other contemporaries were probably as intelligent and perceptive; but I never met another man like him. I don't believe anyone could have been with him for any length of time without being both entranced and the better for it.

He influenced me not frequently but deeply. He was persuasive. He was both charming and honest, two qualities not commonly found in the same person, although he did permit himself an occasional exaggeration as any honest Irishman should. I trust that both God and the Progressive Conservative Party have forgiven him for suggesting to me in 1967 that it was my duty to seek the national leadership of my party. I very early forgave him and was content to enjoy his friendship. With me he was always generous, but he could be bluntly critical. I suspect he treated other party leaders in much the same way.

He was eloquent, but he was capable of missing an air flight absent-mindedly and being some hours late, which could create problems. As a practising politician he had limited success, having run as a candidate only once and being trounced, and not to my knowledge having had much more success as an adviser to other campaigners.

And yet this man was on the Hill or just below the Hill from 1911 to 1976 as a reporter, commentator, editor, and senator. He watched and knew Laurier, Borden, Meighen, King, Bennett, St. Laurent, Diefenbaker, Pearson, Trudeau, and many others. I don't know how much any of these men followed his advice specifically or accepted his criticism, and yet they all worked in a town and in an environment which was influenced daily by the pen, tongue, and above all, the personality of Grattan O'Leary. In this city of struggle, manoeuvre, and endless talk, it is wonderful that through all those sixty-five years there lived here this passionate little Irishman from the Gaspé who cared nothing about personal power for himself, although he never let anyone tramp on him, who fought fiercely for what he believed to be right, who always recognized the difference between persuasion and manipulation, and who knew hog-wash when he saw it.

How lucky we were to have had him here, and how lucky we are now to have these memoirs.

ROBERT L. STANFIELD

INTRODUCTION
by I. Norman Smith

Grattan O'Leary requested that the reader should be told how it came about that he wrote his first and only book at the ages of eighty-seven and eighty-eight, and latterly under the cloud of cancer. His publishers shared that view. I hope I can do it in a way that reveals his spirit in those years.

"Tell them frankly why it is like it is. I was going to use the tapes as notes to rewrite and fill out; and there is so much I never got around to at all." That was on a grey wet-snow day in February 1976, a day of uncharacteristic anxiety. The cold damp along the Rideau River below set the room's mood, though the thermostat was high. He may have sensed he had only two months left.

Ten months earlier he had learned that terminal cancer might strike in a year — and it did, on April 7, 1976. But the anxiety of that February day was not for his health. He had from the outset accepted the doctor's sentence and would not let despair have the last word. It was the book he was anxious about — with little reason.

"I put it off too long," he reflected. He had put it off a dozen years because to write a book was to look back, and his nature was to look ahead. Early in 1963, after O'Leary had entered the Senate and retired as editor of the *Journal*, aged seventy-five, John M. Gray, then president of Macmillan, had begun a long campaign to get him to write his autobiography. Whenever Gray came to Ottawa they would have a noontime or evening full of good talk. The last drink was always to the book. Between times Gray used me as a local spur.

I too pleaded, and assured him the *Journal* would provide re-search and facilities. We had occasional assurance he was getting on with it, but with an Irish twinkle. In 1966 Gray used the ploy of having him sign a contract, but before long O'Leary returned his advance against royalties because his conscience was bothering him.

In Ottawa in those years it wasn't hard to see why he wasn't writing a book. He was a combative member of the Senate, in and out of session, a diligent help in committees, a man whom both Tory and Liberal governments sent abroad on foreign and inter-parliamentary affairs. He once wrote me: "I seem to have lived too long; everyone descends upon me for help in writing *their* book (or doing their broadcast or interview). One day it's a daughter of an old friend writing a thesis on Meighen, another an academic doing research on Laurier, the next someone working on C. D. Howe." That was but a tenth of it. He would travel anywhere to speak for a friend running for Parliament, would attend Communion breakfasts, anniversaries, weddings, and funerals, and argue his body and heart out on platform and television in his concern for parliamentary democracy.

The years went by until in January 1973 he told me "there will be no book". He said he had done nothing. Solo and in duet Gray and I implored, but he was firm. He was, after all, almost eighty-five years old, and had lived them hard. He bore the misery of shingles, a "back", and recurring arthritis. "I'm tired," he sighed.

In the light of this, having retired some months earlier, I thought then of doing a little memoir of my predecessors on the *Journal*: P. D. Ross, E. Norman Smith, and M. Grattan O'Leary. I felt someone should get their lives down, and Grattan spurred me to it, including talking to me on tapes.

Seven months later, in much better health and spirit, he told me he had been persuaded by Peter Dobell to work on his book, and to have Tom Van Dusen get down his political recollections. This was great news. Hugh Kane, now in charge at Macmillan, carried on Gray's earlier encouragement. But O'Leary hadn't changed. Still wanting to live today and not yesterday, he gave his talks with Van Dusen a low priority. Besides, this unique journalist, speaker, and book-lover was nervous about doing his book. He might never have "finished" it even had he started years earlier. Those who knew him only as a fiery political fighter would not sense his modesty and humility.

On April 10, 1975, Grattan phoned to say he was not well. I went right over. That morning he had fallen while getting out of bed. Though in pain, he had gone down to the Senate anyway, but was obliged to have x-rays and was now at home awaiting the results.

"I think perhaps I have torn some ligaments, but that's not important. My doctor has told me I have a malignant tumor on my lung, terminal cancer, a year to eighteen months." Grattan told me this quietly, without drama. His doctor, a great personal friend (Dr. C. B. Petrie), told him he should keep on doing things, even the out-of-town speaking engagements Grattan wanted to keep. But he must not get tired. "Everyone tells me that, the family too. For God's sake, I don't want to take it easy. The only thing I'm worried about is my book. I am not going to be able to finish it."

I suggested his worrying was about the labour of editing, proof-reading, and production, which he could leave to the house of Macmillan. In the meantime he should put on tape those things he most wanted to do, and if he gave them half an hour a day he'd have it all off his mind in three months. "I've got eighteen months," he grinned; but then with a touch of his old mischief he asked me if I would edit it. I told him Macmillan should edit the book if he couldn't, that my being editor would be bad for the book. I reminded him that over the years he had held that close friends or relatives should not edit a man's life story. "Everyone knows I practically cross myself every time I mention your name." He smiled agreement, and we talked of other things, of everything but cancer. But once out of the building I had a rough time of it.

O'Leary did try to turn more intently to the book, but concentration was hard for him. General weakness was now added to a tearing cough, and he was easy prey to colds. One in June developed into pneumonia that might have taken him right then. But never mind that, down he went in a wheel chair to a large farewell dinner in his honour on Parliament Hill! Prime Minister

Trudeau, Robert Stanfield, and others, spoke with respect and admiration of the Senator's unique character and distinction; and under Gordon Fairweather's graceful chairmanship there was the sense of occasion of a state banquet, yet the intimate, poignant air of a last reunion of friends. In his brief response Grattan spoke with affectionate concern of Canada and of democracy. An almost reverent hush and then standing acclaim followed his last sentences:

> Now I come to my years. Old age does not flavour of enchantment. The best you can do is to think of those adorable lines from Emily Brontë when she spoke of old age as "when winds take on a pensive note and stars a tender fire". My old comrades with whom I have marched and tented over the years, yes, and old antagonists with whom I have fought over the years, thank you all for coming here. God bless you and God bless Canada.

Exhaustion followed, but then he went down to the sea at White Point Beach, Nova Scotia, among friends and memories, the salt air, the sand, the spruce, and the waves. He loved the sea. Looking out brightly from among the sober-covered books in his library at home had stood, in a small frame, a poem of Ada Enright O'Sullivan, "Gaspé-born". It opened with these lines:

> If you are Gaspé born, you know
> The rhythmic song of breaking waves
> The brooding quiet—prelude to snow
> Along the Gaspé shores; you listen
> For honking wild geese in November,
> A seabird's forlorn cry in Spring
> No day goes by but you remember . . .

It was a long, fact-facing fall. His reaching out to life was shortened, his open house less open; the poker nights, and the evenings of good talk at his unique "dining-out club", were no more. But he remained the cheery host; solicitous of visitors, asking of their doings and their friends. In November and De-

cember he was in hospital to "take the bomb", said he with sceptical eye. Several times as I left his hospital room I thought I had
seen him for the last time. But he rallied, and by Christmas he had
all his family and his dog for a three-day reunion at the Château
Laurier! It played him out, as he knew it would, but he loved it,
even the fatigue.

The book remained at the top of his mind, disturbingly. He had
misgivings about the quality of the tapes he had done for Van
Dusen. Scarcely a month before he died, speaking of his book to
Patrick Watson in a wide-ranging CBC interview, Grattan said:
"I've never dictated. . . . I spoil all my stuff when I dictate and I've
got to do it all over again. You see, I write by ear . . . I write a line
. . . did it sound all right when I read it over? . . . You can't do that
when you're dictating. You're trying to make a speech and a good
speech is not good writing."

I knew nothing of the O'Leary–Van Dusen work, but later on
Tom told me of those sessions in O'Leary's Senate office: how he
began by just taking notes, then using tapes; how the interviews
did not follow any sequential form. Tom recalled it this way: "He
dealt largely with political events because he wanted to get them
out of the way, hoping to turn to personal matters later. No one
knew better than he that the material could not go in as delivered,
and no one is more aware than I of the deficiencies. Somehow, in
spite of the difficulties, I think the result is substantially Grattan.
Though often in discomfort, he had incredible cheerfulness, toler-
ation, and will to fight. He was always very kind to me. Working
with him was a tremendous privilege."

Well, O'Leary was certainly grateful for Tom's work and
kindness, and for Peter Dobell's initial role. Tom regrets the
"deficiencies", but I well know that O'Leary's flow of convictions,
damnings, and exhortations could not easily be guided. Tom decided to let the words run free and see later what was to be done.
Time and health ran out on Grattan, but only in the sense that he
was unable to revise it to his sense of "perfection", a goal he
always believed should be just beyond us all!

It was mid-January 1976 when he shooed the nurse (how fortunate he was in his nurses and how they adored him!) out of the

room and asked me to take home the typescript. I got it from a cupboard, all 412 pages stuck together by their electricity, un-thumbed. "I haven't read it; please read it and give me a frank report. I'm not even sure there's a book at all." He said nothing else about it, but eyed the pile with mixed emotions.

Within a few days I bustled over and told him with genuine enthusiasm that of course there was a book there. I said it needed some editing but that would be largely a matter of transplanting, cutting, and good gardening, not of writing. He seemed relieved, yet asked plaintively what of the several matters he had yet to write on and must write on; "will you help me with those?" Naturally I said I would. It was not difficult to find enough of his own words, for I had for over forty years saved his office memos, speeches, and articles by and about him, and I have most of his correspondence. We put on tapes some of our conversation on matters not covered. When I read to him, several times and slowly, the half-dozen pages I had put together he said quietly: "Those are my thoughts, even my words."

So the way ahead was clear. He asked me to send it all off to Macmillan, with some comments I had made to him on things their editors might keep in mind. I took care to send them the entire typescript so they could see and edit it whole; my questions or comments were in the margins. A few days later my phone rang with what seemed unusual urgency. It was Grattan, calling out with youthful excitement, as though trying to be heard above the surf: "Norman, I've heard from Macmillan and we're all set; Kane has written me a wonderful letter, a lovely letter, really. Now I can relax."

John Gray, on reading the typescript after Grattan died, wrote me of an exchange he had with O'Leary in the sixties, when he was coaxing him to write his book: "He confessed he had done nothing—yet. With a rush of candour that was somehow painful, he added: 'I'm afraid of writing a bad book.' I answered with more truth than I knew: 'You couldn't write a bad book if you tried; you might write a less good book than you hoped, many people do that, but you couldn't write a bad book.'"

John Gray was right. Had Grattan had time he might have

honed some of his recollections and judgments, but I know at the end he wanted it all to stand, unrevised and unrepented, as did Meighen's autobiography. There is no ghost-writing here; but there is beautiful writing, as in this glance back at Ireland:

> I have often stayed at a little inn at Adair, during the war full of R.A.F. officers in mufti. There is an old castle there and an old church and a bar and winding Irish roads and Irish faces and Irish speech, and it is like coming home.

Grattan charged me that this introduction must not make him out to be a cross between Jesus Christ and Abraham Lincoln. But there was a little bit of both in him, and of the Old Nick. I wish only that he had had time to write more of the personal things which meant so much to him. Religion, courtesy, caring, curiosity, youth, sports, laughter, and respect. He was aware his book was long on politics: "There's not enough warmth in that thing," he grumbled. For that reason, yet hesitantly, I have written a postscript, warmed by his own lively words and those of his friends, which I hope conveys something of the nature and atmosphere of the man.

REMEMBERED HILLS

It was the Golden Age of Victorianism — 1888. London was the capital of the world. Robert Arthur Talbot Gascoyne-Cecil, third Marquess of Salisbury, presided over the destiny of the Empire on which even the sun hadn't the temerity to set. Fourteen years remained of Victoria's imperishable reign. In Canada, bastion of Empire, John A. Macdonald was heading for his last election. A young man by the name of Wilfrid Laurier had been chosen to succeed the great Edward Blake as leader of the Liberal Party. Louis Riel, whose obscure followers had for a time impeded the march of progress across the Prairies, lay cold in his grave in the St. Boniface churchyard.

I chose this propitious moment to be plummeted into the world in an obscure pocket of Empire, the Irish settlement of Gaspé, where Percé Rock thrust its improbable buttress up from the shining sea. Amid loneliness and terrible beauty and searing poverty. Barren farms tumbling down to the sea provided a bare living for those with stark memories of the "Great Hunger" in a land they had left behind. Enfilading the coast with battalions of sleet and snow, winter storms came roaring up out of the sea, paralysing movement, throwing us on our slender resources.

The Irish of Gaspé, a little bit of the old land: winter evenings round the stove, talk slow and deep of the land they had left behind; the names on the Irishtown Road like the roll-call of the brigades whose tread shook the pages of history. Soldiers from Wolfe's army got land grants along the harsh, rock-girt coast. The O'Learys came later in the wake of Napoleon's war, old soldiers turned to fishing and farming along the Irishtown Road. The

misted hills knew Irish tears and Irish laughter, the names remembered on headstones in the village churchyard, faded now
almost beyond deciphering in years of wind and weather.

On one of those headstones was the name of my own mother,
dead of a wasting illness when I was scarcely a year old, her
likeness beyond the reach of memory. My father's second wife
was the only mother I ever knew, a good woman and kindly, but
too taken up with endless chores to be aware of a lonely boy.

Often the exiles' thoughts turned to Ireland; no nation so long
holds the affection of its sons and daughters. Flung by the "Great
Famine" to the sea, their ancient language lost, unlettered and
poor, they sang the ballads that were the nurslings of memory,
kept Patrick's Day, had less than love for England.

For the English I hold no animosity. They have been my friends,
and true friends in every clime. The worst that can be said of them
is that they are prisoners of their history and their pride. Once
removed from Irish soil (which I, incidentally, have visited
twenty-four times), an Irishman should leave ancient hatreds
where they can do no harm, in the coffers of eternity. No more
bitter alchemy in my years than the spectacle of Irishmen, hatred
in their hearts, cruelly murdering and destroying other Irish over
the dismal chimera of religious difference.

In Irishtown we did have a few non-Catholic people, mostly
from the islands of Jersey and Guernsey. They had a little church,
St. Paul's Anglican church. I can see it in memory now, standing
on a hill overlooking the sea, surrounded by elms and weeping
willows. This was a mission church. The minister came to preach
to these few people once every month. And I recall very well that
every spring my father and the fathers of the other Irish Roman
Catholic boys in that bay would send us down to do one or two
days of free work fixing up the lawn of the Anglican church,
replanting the flowerbeds, trimming the hedges, and pruning the
shrubs. We never thought that this wasn't the due course of
things; it never occurred to us that we were doing anything very
noble or unique. These were our neighbours.

Our farm stretched back from the sea, one hundred acres under
cultivation, another hundred in bush. In our house three pictures
held pride of place: the Pope, Parnell, and John L. Sullivan, exiles

and their descendants clinging to belief in the glory of religion and race. The horror racing through the Irish settlement at the news of John L.'s defeat was only moderately allayed by the word that the man Corbett, who beat him, was an Irishman too.

My father talked of Parnell and Gladstone more than he did of Macdonald or Laurier; and of the wrongs and sorrows of Ireland, Dublin with its "memoried sorrow and old renown" more after his heart than Ottawa, Quebec, or Montreal. I was given my father's name of Michael at baptism, taking the name of the hero of Ireland's Great Parliament at my confirmation, along with a love of Irish letters and Irish freedom.

There was hardship and privation on a Gaspé farm at the turn of the century; there were also compensations. The magic of an upland meadow in the dusk, sheep tracks winding across one brow of a hill; sunlight glinting on the silver sea. In the measured days I learned the rhythm of reaping and threshing; spun wool for homespun we produced on our own loom; made boots from our own leather. Self-sufficiency could ask little more.

There was no unemployment insurance, no welfare except what the parish could find in its heart and pockets to give; no medicare. A bell summoned the workers in the grey dawn to trawl out fish to be dried on the flakes; they worked on until dusk, sometimes as late as midnight, for about seventy-five cents a day. You could buy a quart of milk for ten cents.

There was little to hope for from outside resources, particularly government; the harsh, lonely life compelled self-reliance, a capacity for dreams and longings not learned from the television screen. Happy I was to walk three miles to the village store, the sea wind cutting like a knife, selling eggs for ten cents a dozen, butter for fifteen cents a pound.

Linking us with the mysterious world beyond the headlands, the sea brought barks and brigantines lured by Gaspé's cod — great, shining fish lurking off our shores. Beauty there was in craggy cliffs thrusting headlands to the sea; years later on a Hawaiian beach, the moon rising over the Pacific in mystic grandeur could not match the compelling beauty of remembered hills, seabirds clustered in clouds round Percé Rock.

Events from the world outside were brought to our doors by

newspapers which arrived at particularly long intervals in winter, breaking the monotony of our days and nights with their welcome cargo of information about famous men and great events. From New York came the *Irish World*, calling for the dynamiting of everything English; not far behind was the *Gaelic American* with John Devoy, the last and greatest Fenian, as editor. The *Montreal Star* came with news of Laurier's third and greatest victory. To my elders who lacked schooling I was called on to read by candlelight round the kitchen stove. Correspondents like Winston Churchill, the son of the great Lord Randolph, and Richard Harding Davis gave to remote battles of Boer and Briton the urgency of high drama. The Irish of Gaspé, though, lined up solidly with the gallant people who dared to stand up to the Empire's might.

> Brave General De Wet,
> Sure you lick all creation;
> To the redcoats you're causing
> The utmost vexation
> And bringing such shame
> On the great British nation!
> More power to your elbow
> Brave General De Wet!

Thus, the gossoons of the Irish settlement chanting the rhymes that showed there was never a friend of the redcoats along the Irishtown Road.

Then as now there was precious little peace in the world: Russia and Japan locked in conflict in the Far East; Briton and Boer disputing the sovereignty of the Transvaal; the United States chastising Spain for her oppression of "brave little Cuba". Though the guns were far off and faint, we managed to follow Dewey in Manila Bay ("You may fire when ready, Gridley") and Roberts and Kitchener in South Africa.

They live on in memory's pages, those evenings when the woodstove filled the kitchen with pulsing heat in

... solitude made more intense
By dreary voiced elements,
The shrieking of the mindless wind,
The moaning tree boughs swaying blind,
And on the glass the unmeaning beat
Of ghostly finger-tips of sleet.

A Gaspé kitchen at the century's turn; memories that in the lengthening and faded track of life may blur but never die.

Early I gained the advantage of a few books carefully digested, grateful for the relief of intellectual penury offered by the sister of a scholarly priest. Education used to mean communication with great minds; now it has become the absorption of petty theories. Since I was not exposed to outpourings of trivia, the fascination of great words, great ideas, was engraved on my mind. With the night wind scratching at the eaves, by the flickering candle I eagerly absorbed the exploits of Wallace and Bruce in that authoritative compendium of Scottish grandeur, *The Scottish Chiefs*; I sharpened my controversial bent on the sermons of DeWitt Talmadge and became a devotee of Justin McCarthy's *A History of Our Own Times*; I was captured by the ring and glitter of Macaulay's sonorous prose. At twelve, formal education finished, I departed the one-room Percé schoolhouse.

Amid the screeching of saws and blizzard of sawdust in a local mill, my destiny appeared decided. Like many others without education or prospects, I would move from job to job until too old to work any more. It turned out that destiny had other plans. The occasion was my going to sea as an engine-room helper on a newly built coastal ship, the *Lady Eileen*, named for the daughter of the Governor General, Lord Minto.

I worked as an oiler for the splendid wage of fifteen dollars a month; never before or since have I worked so hard for the money I earned. Thrown in with the job was the privilege of reading in the forecastle by the single electric bulb, the first I'd ever seen. In our cramped, poorly ventilated quarters, which were down below the water line when the ship was loaded, we could hear the water swishing against the planking.

Amenities were non-existent; no showers or radios, none of the things today deemed indispensable for the well-ordered pursuit of a seafaring vocation. Ship's biscuit, hardtack, cold pork, and tea rounded out our bill of fare. I do not recommend it to anyone accustomed to the delicacies of the Parliamentary Restaurant. One can imagine the reaction of today's welfare recipients.

My first voyage ended in disaster when our cargo of bagged pulp shifted in a heavy gale off New England, springing a loading-door and allowing water to pour in. Soon the ship was rolling heavily and we were jettisoning cargo to lighten her. The floor of the stokehold was inches deep in water and the Chief Engineer, a Saint John man named Currie, ordered the bunker doors closed to keep the water out of the coal.

We had to have coal for the furnaces, and the Chief hit on the expedient of lowering me, as the youngest and lightest member of the crew, into the bunker on the end of a rope; the idea was that I should scoop up pailfuls of coal between rolls of the ship. The water in the bunker ran from one side to the other; with each roll of the vessel I disappeared momentarily to emerge coughing and spluttering. The situation began to look black when the Captain sent word to abandon; he was, of course, staying. The Chief Engineer was determined to stay with the ship, as were the two Assistant Engineers, Scotsmen both. Not to be outdone by three Scots, I said I too would stay. The feelings with which I watched the boats pull away in the spume-driven darkness were anything but heroic. By some miracle the *Lady Eileen* got through the night.

What was our surprise in the turbulence of uncertain dawn to see the boats returning; the crew, lost amid the raging seas, simply rowed round in a circle and came back, glad to take their chances with the *Lady Eileen.* Made buoyant by the bags of wood pulp in her hold, she managed to make it to the William Cramp and Sons yards in Philadelphia for repairs.

Philadelphia was a city of heavenly light, storefronts blazing with Christmas decorations like Aladdin's cave. At home our only Christmas lights were penny candles, and not many of those. I got my pay and went downtown, spending more than I could afford on newspapers and books. I came back to the ship and made coffee with water from the boilers and, grateful for their warmth, sat there reading while the crew went out on the town.

Other voyages were less eventful. Then came a series of port-side jobs: brewery worker in Saint John, lathe operator, clerk for a wholesale hardware merchant, sales clerk for a lumber concern run by a distant relative in Richibucto.

One day a man came in—the smiling stranger of legend—and asked me to help load a wagon with steel rods. There was, he said, no need to make out a sales slip since he was a member of the firm. Unfortunately, he was nothing of the kind, nor did we ever see him again. I was sent out of harm's way to Logieville on the Miramichi, a sad example of the Alger story in reverse; already at a tender age a complete failure in the business world.

Back in Saint John I haunted the harbour, hoping amid the forest of masts to find a berth. I found a ship readying for South Africa and was told to come down and sign on the following day. Walking back to my room I was struck by a sign announcing the editorial office of the *Saint John Standard*, a newspaper for which I had considerable respect since it and I were both Conservative.

It was the sort of impulsive thing a young fellow does. I decided to ask for a job; I had never written a line but I had read a lot and was convinced I could write well enough to fill a column of the paper's closely set type. Up the rickety stairs to the second floor I went and found the editor in his sanctum, ready to go home, an impressive, almost Jovian figure in a green eyeshade. He turned a languid countenance on me as I explained that I had the makings of a writer.

"Have you done any reporting?"

"No, but I'm a good Conservative."

For the first time he seemed impressed. He looked me over carefully and told me to go out and find a story and bring it back for the night editor. "Tell him Mr. Scott sent you." This was S. D. Scott, the great Conservative editor who later went to the *Vancouver Province* and became a power on the West Coast.

I went down the stairs filled with zeal and made my way to the harbour. I might not know much about reporting, but I knew something about ships. In the pilotage office I obtained the figures on traffic in the port which, at that time, was being touted by Sir

7

Wilfrid Laurier's Minister of Public Works, William Pugsley, as the "Liverpool of America". It wasn't quite that, but the figures indicated that traffic in Saint John had taken a healthy upswing. I sat down in the pilotage office and wrote the story in longhand, dropping it off at the *Standard* office on my way home. I was packing for my departure when I was called to the telephone. It was the night editor of the *Standard*. Mr. Scott liked my work and wanted to see me in the morning. South Africa went glimmering.

APPRENTICESHIP

Saint John, New Brunswick, 1909. A bustling maritime port. Steam had taken over the sea lanes and rusty tramps and coastal steamers predominated in the harbour; here and there amid the smokestacks the tall masts of a sailing ship riding at anchor. Nautical figures roamed narrow portside streets and filled the grog shops. It was a town well served by newspapers. In addition to the *Standard*, Saint John boasted the *Telegraph*, the *Globe*, the *Morning Sun*, the *Evening Star*, and the *Forum*, and the *New Freeman* for Irish Readers. The *New Freeman* was edited by a doughty priest called Father O'Keefe who, without a note, was able to lecture a hall packed with members of the Ancient Order of Hibernians on the life and achievements of O'Connell.

Apart from such diversions, and the limited amenities of the local library, Saint John was a cultural wilderness. I covered fires, attended court, recorded ship arrivals and departures, met incoming trains, and religiously greeted the arrival of the boat from Boston each evening as it discharged its cargo of trippers on the Saint John pier. I became acquainted with local politicians and got to know something of what made the wheels go round in municipal politics. It was a cheap education; I enjoyed being able to write and get paid for doing it. A good fire was the highlight of a reporter's life, provided, of course, there was no loss of life. Fire engines were drawn by spanking teams of matched horses; equipment was burnished to sparkling perfection. Transportation was by rail or water or carriage — and carriages had only recently become horseless. The railways played a great part in people's lives. Day coaches had wicker or plush-covered seats. Dining cars were well appointed with gleaming napery and sparkling silver. For the well-to-do travelling by night, there were palatial Pullman cars. All the cars in the country seemed to converge on Saint John.

Competition among the papers was intense. The rule was no fraternization; while reporters from rival papers got together for a cup of coffee or something stronger, they didn't hesitate to cut one another's throats for a "scoop". Personal journalism was not yet on the wane. Great names like T. P. O'Connor, James Gordon Bennett, Jr., William Randolph Hearst, Richard Harding Davis, and Charles Dana, shone forth in the star-studded sky of contemporary journalism, surrounded by all the glamour of today's TV stars. In England a youth called Winston Churchill, having made a name in journalism, was trying to match his father's fame in politics. In western Canada, Nicholas Flood Davin, the man who had covered Louis Riel's hanging, set a standard of reporting equal to any. In Ottawa P. D. Ross was making a name.

S. D. Scott, the editor of the *Standard*, was a distinguished upholder of Conservative principles on a paper owned by the Conservative Party. He was never biased or unfair. His patrician appearance, as well as the power of his writing, gave him a legendary air. In the shabby editorial room of the old *Standard* he seemed a high priest of journalism as he went about the business of defending the bastions of Conservatism.

Politics was both a way of life and a fascinating diversion. The Liberal Member for Saint John, William Pugsley, a gifted lawyer, more than held his own in later years with Elihu Root and Joseph Choate, America's best. Political meetings drew large crowds and oratory waxed fast and furious. People turned out in droves for Robert Borden or Wilfrid Laurier.

For two years I apprenticed my trade, living in a boarding house, taking my meals as often as not at an all-night coffee-and-bean wagon, a Boston innovation along the lines of Britain's fish-and-chips carts. My City Editor, a man named McGinley, a grand old Orangeman, a grand orator, a great Tory and a grand drinker, told me that P. D. Ross up in Ottawa was looking for a young reporter for his paper, the *Ottawa Journal*.

"For all the good you're doing here," he said, "you might as well be up there." It was his homely way of offering me opportunity. I borrowed enough money from him for train fare and was on my way.

After sitting up all night because I couldn't afford the price of a sleeper, I arrived in Ottawa at one o'clock the following afternoon, emerging from the splendour of the Union Station to gaze entranced at the towers of Parliament, the magnificence of the Russell Hotel and the Russell Theatre, the architectural marvel that was the Sappers' Bridge, beneath which the Rideau Canal slid like a muddy brown snake.

In 1911 the city was a bit of Bytown, still a lumber village. The old Russell Hotel, with its potted palms, shining brass spittoons, and businessman's lunch for one dollar, was the social centre. Government House was a shore perceived but dimly. Rivalry abounded between the remaining lumber barons and the new breed of public servants over invitations to Government House. The Civil Service élite had not yet reached its flower. The Department of External Affairs was in its infancy. Glamorous and highly visible departments such as Health and Welfare, Supply and Services, and Environment, were not imagined. Crown corporations with their almost unlimited disposal of huge budgets were not even a gleam in the eye of political theorizers.

It was a colonial atmosphere. When Canada had sent a thousand men to South Africa a few years earlier, Lord Minto forwarded the government's timid suggestion that they be kept together in these words:

> They should, if at all possible be kept together but . . . my Ministers . . . realize that this must be left to the discretion of the War Office and Commander in Chief.

With what contrasting vehemence only a few years later Sir Sam Hughes was to insist on the right of Canadians in the First World War to be kept in autonomous units within the imperial forces.

The Duke of Connaught held sway at Rideau Hall with all the panoply of a distinguished military career in Egypt and India, clothed in the aura of Queen Victoria's third son. The Governor

General had his office in the East Block, reached through a porte-cochère and a red-carpeted stairway. As head of the Council, he was far from the supernumerary he became following the constitutional confrontation between Mackenzie King and Lord Byng, a situation in which honour, decency, and right were on Byng's side and deceit, demagoguery, and victory on King's. The doughty soldier under whose command the Canadians stormed Vimy Ridge in 1917 had little taste for political intrigue.

Viscount Alexander, another in the line of distinguished British soldiers, did much to rid the office of the trappings of ceremony and, paradoxical as it may seem, to "Canadianize" it. Vincent Massey, a Canadian, was more British than the British. Curiously, while British holders of the office showed ability to adapt its subtleties to changing times, Canadians have clung to protocol or reduced the office to the level of travelling ambassador to the hinterlands.

In later years Colonel H. Willis O'Connor, the viceregal aide-de-camp, was known to complain discreetly about the way in which precedence-conscious Ottawa socialites made his telephone leap from its cradle with complaints about the order in which they had been seated at the viceregal table. Many of those who complained most bitterly had as much claim to precedence as Paddy's pig.

When I arrived in Ottawa, it was a slow-paced, leisurely world, close to us in time but infinitely removed by the acceleration of change. The Rideau Club, today so democratized as to allow entry to mere government employees, was in those days a bastion of privilege reserved for the hierarchy of birth and command which Ottawa, emerging from the Bytown chrysalis, prided itself on reflecting.

An outpost of Empire, stuffy with colonialism. That was Ottawa. Yet it was a comfortable kind of colonialism for those fortunate enough to have a place in the little hierarchy of Wellington Street. The old families — English, Northern Irish, Scottish, with a sprinkling of lace-curtain Irish — liked it the way it was. The French in their Lower Town ghetto didn't seem to care. Few French were members of the Rideau Club; few appeared to worry about it. Fewer still got into the Country Club. Ottawa, like Ireland, had its Pale, but it was an invisible one.

The working Irish, descendants of those brought by Colonel By to build the canal, dwelt cheek by jowl with the French in Lower Town or filtered out to the surrounding countryside. Beer was twenty-five cents a pail and jobs were good on the railway and the rivers. When jobs were scarce the Irish and French would fly at each other's throats. A backwater of the world, Ottawa was an intellectual waste saved only by the pens of Archibald Lampman, Duncan Campbell Scott, and Bliss Carman.

It was not the Union Jack that flew over the East Block but the royal standard, signifying that the Governor General was in his office and all was right with the world. The idea of a Canadian flag was practically a breath of treason and a word against Queen Victoria was an invitation to capital punishment.

The newspapers were hopelessly parochial. London was our spiritual home, and if it rained in the Strand we turned up our trouser legs on Sparks Street. As for bilingualism, I don't think the word was invented.

On that first day, instead of going immediately to the *Ottawa Journal* I directed my steps to Parliament, the repository of the nation's destiny, the arena where I lost myself for the afternoon gazing and listening in awe while political giants locked in forensic combat: Laurier's famous silver plume, his gestures like a man playing a delicate instrument; Borden, restrained, solid seriousness. I stayed until the lamps sprang up and I suddenly realized I had a job waiting.

I hastened to the corner of Elgin and Sparks streets where the *Journal*, not yet merged with E. Norman Smith's *Ottawa Free Press*, was located. In the gathering dusk I took a long, last look at the Parliament Buildings. Mr. Ross had just about given me up.

EARLY YEARS AT THE JOURNAL

My weekly salary of seventeen dollars was only two dollars more than I had been getting in Saint John; something I had forgotten to ask about before starting for Ottawa. The *Journal*'s circulation was about ten thousand. Money was hard to find. On pay-days P. D. Ross went to the bank and signed a note for money to pay the staff. It would not always be like this.

My early assignments were of a routine nature; yet from each one I managed to learn something of the workings of the elusive medium of journalism. I was assigned to cover a tightly closed and highly volatile meeting of the congregation of a prominent Presbyterian church in Ottawa. The purpose was to fire the minister and no reporters were allowed in. I managed to breach the tight security by assuming a pious expression and walking in with the trustees. I knew that my Managing Editor, Mr. George Wilson, a staunch member of the congregation, was deeply interested in the outcome.

When I returned with my story, several columns detailing the clash of factions within the church, Mr. Wilson read it with an expression of acute and mournful interest and proceeded to tear it in little pieces and drop it into his wastebasket, shaking his head sorrowfully. It was a rather shocking introduction to the great principle of free and unfettered comment.

In 1911 James Muir was brought down from the Press Gallery to be Managing Editor and after a month I was sent to replace him. The Press Gallery before the First World War was a cosy little enclave. Arthur Hannay represented the *Ottawa Free Press*, Harry Anderson the Toronto *Globe*, Tom Blacklock several newspapers, and John Stevenson the London *Times*. Sir John Willison's Toronto *News* had C. F. Hamilton of Boer War fame. The big American papers were represented. Among the twenty or twenty-five Gallery members there was a camaraderie difficult to find today. Being appointed to the Parliamentary Press Gallery was, of course, a tremendous honour, like an appointment to the Senate. More than any other press corps, the Gallery enjoys a privileged position in the affairs of the nation. In those days the Press Gallery, like the Prime Minister's office, was on the ground floor of the Centre Block.

The Commons boasted a bar which accounted in part for the fine, free flow of language in the press and in the House. One called up the shades of Macdonald and McGee and Tupper and J. J. C. Abbott gathering for a nightcap after the House rose. From just such a scene, no doubt, Thomas D'Arcy McGee, the greatest Irishman in Canadian history, wended his way home in the early hours of April 6, 1868, having delivered one of his most masterly speeches, only to be brought down in his own blood by the pistol of the Fenian, Whelan. When the cold hand of prohibition closed the bar, something went out of the House.

My first important assignment for the *Journal* was in connection with the sinking of the *Titanic*, the greatest, most modern ship of its time, deemed unsinkable by its builders. I was told to go to New York and interview the survivors on their way to port in the s.s. *Carpathia*. The assignment was not a tribute to my reporting ability but was based on the assumption that because I had spent several years at sea I was well qualified to interview survivors of a shipwreck.

I arrived in New York in early evening, an April night of teeming rain. I stayed at the Breslin, operated by a relative of the manager of the Russell Hotel in Ottawa. There were extras on the street saying the *Carpathia* wouldn't dock until the following morning, so I enjoyed a leisurely dinner with a couple of cocktails, only to find, when I came out in the street, that a later extra contradicted the earlier one and the *Carpathia* was on the point of discharging her cargo of pitiful survivors.

I was anxious to get down to the docks and get the story, one of the most gripping of the day. When I arrived at the dock area it was crowded with thousands of people eager to see those who had escaped the most dramatic sea catastrophe in history. I had no police pass, and without it there was no way of getting through. I took a taxi to Associated Press, told the night editor who I was and what I was there for, and got his assurance that the first reporter to return from the docks would allow me the use of his pass. Associated Press had forty people out on the story that night and one of them was bound to come in at any moment. Sure enough, in about fifteen minutes a reporter came into the office and, good as his word, the night editor, an upstanding Irishman, took the badge off his own man and turned it over to me. In a few minutes I was on my way through tight-packed crowds miserable in the rain, many of them hoping for word of loved ones.

I stood by the gangplank and interviewed the survivors as they stumbled into the arms of waiting friends and relatives, a touching and moving scene.

My story appeared in the *Ottawa Journal* of Friday, April 19, 1912.

> ...The uniforms of two hundred nurses and Red Cross attaches mingled in the picture with the trim garbs of the ambulance surgeons and the chaste costumes of sad faced sisters of charity. Ten score city policemen guarded the rope cordon lighted up at intervals with green lanterns whereby the guardians of the city's peace kept back at a distance of seventy-five feet the throng that kept pressing over-eagerly toward the pier where the Carpathia was docked.
>
> Within the shelter of the pier sheds were huddled nearly a thousand of the friends and relatives of the rescued and the lost. Many of them were weeping and sobbing without restraint. Outside in the murk and drizzle of the forbidding night stood ominous lines of ambulances to which nearly all the hospitals in the city had contributed their quota. . . .

If you ask me whether I would write the same way today, the answer is, of course, no. Things were different then. Reporters were not competing against the ubiquitous television screen, which brings the actual event with its sights and sounds into people's living rooms. You had to fill in; you had to supply details for which the popular imagination hungered feverishly. Thus was born a school of descriptive writing which, I am afraid, lingers on only in memory.

Years later my *Titanic* story was selected as one of the Canadian news stories of the century; not bad for a Gaspé boy whose schooling stopped at twelve. I often think how fortunate I was to escape the soul-destroying impact of post-secondary education.

An aftermath of the story was the suit launched by P. D. Ross against the Ottawa *Citizen*. The *Citizen* had sent Tommy Gorman to New York, a junior reporter then, later a nationally known sports promoter. Being unable to get through the police lines to the dock where the *Carpathia* was discharging passengers, Tommy didn't have a word from the survivors. Somehow the *Citizen* got the idea they'd been outfoxed, and in order to cover up their own failure they stated that the *Journal* story was an imaginative exercise, a fraud; that I had never got to the *Carpathia* survivors.

Quite concerned, P. D. called me in. "Can you prove you were at the dock?" I showed him the New York police pass; the *Citizen's* lawyers advised them to print an apology, which they did reluctantly.

It wasn't long before P. D. was once more threatening a suit in connection with one of my stories. On this occasion I had been sent to the United States to get information on various types of water filtration plants, a major issue in Ottawa municipal politics at that time. The city had come through a typhoid epidemic and the city fathers determined there should never be another. They made up their minds to install a water-purifying plant. The *Citizen*, because of the Christian Science convictions of the owners, the Southam family, was dead set against such interference with natural processes.

By sheer luck I found the Chief Engineer for the State of Massachusetts in the State House in Boston on Christmas Eve. He produced official reports showing that mechanical filtration —one of the methods currently being studied by the City of Ottawa — was not as effective in controlling contamination of water as gravity filtration, advocated by the *Journal*. When this came out, the *Citizen* once again refused to believe I had been to the United

States to obtain the information printed in the story. They accordingly rushed into print denying the truth of my article.

P. D. was not having any of this. Furious, he dashed off a sizzling editorial headed "The Libeler Libels Again". Again he threatened suit, and again, after consultation between lawyers when I was easily able to establish the authenticity of my story, the *Citizen* printed a front-page apology. P. D. always stood by his reporters as long as they could prove they were right, a great quality in an editor.

The Russell Hotel was a regular stamping ground for journalists in those days. Jack O'Brien, the desk man, always gave the high sign when anyone important signed the register. I generally took my post in the high-ceilinged lobby with its dusty palms, gleaming brass cuspidors, and framed paintings of Crimean battles.

I was sitting in the lobby one day, deep in the Toronto *Mail*, when Jack gave me the wigwag. The dapper young man he indicated was Max Aitken, boyhood friend and associate of R. B. Bennett, the second half of a rags-to-riches story which saw two small-town New Brunswick lads climb to dizzy heights, one as a great publisher and wartime minister in Britain, the other as Prime Minister of Canada. Even at this time Max Aitken was someone to be reckoned with, publisher of the London *Daily Express*, one of the Empire's leading journalists, and a major shareholder in the Canada Cement Company. Even without Jack O'Brien's tip-off I should have recognized the ugly, witty, intelligent face. He agreed to give me an interview and invited me up to his room.

At that moment he was in the thick of some controversy with Sir Sandford Fleming, then Chancellor of Queen's University. Naturally I asked him for a comment about the dispute. He said, "No. He's one of the great Canadians: the man who surveyed the Rockies for the c.p.r. and found Kicking Horse Pass, without which the c.p.r. never would have got through. You want me to criticize a man like that in this country? Not on your life." I had to be content with that. I got a good interview anyway, and a couple of days later a box of cigars arrived with Aitken's card. It was my first meeting with Max Aitken but far from my last.

One of the bizarre episodes of the First World War was the Parliament Buildings fire in February 1916. I was at a dinner given by the Minister of Militia, Sir Sam Hughes, at the Château Laurier. His dinners were not dry dinners. There were about eight or ten of us there, and one guest from the north of Ireland had a delightful baritone voice. He was in the middle of singing "Where the Mountains of Mourne Come Down to the Sea" when the door burst open and someone said, "Good God! What are you people doing here? Don't you know the Parliament Buildings are on fire?" We said, "We'll go up and put the fire out shortly. Now go away and don't bother us." But half an hour later someone else came, and then we thought we had better have a look. We streamed out to find a pall of black smoke obscuring Parliament Hill and the main tower of the Centre Block shooting great gouts of flame high in the night.

I dashed into the building to get my typewriter and made my way outside through corridors filled with smoke. By this time a great crowd had gathered. It was a bitterly cold night, and people caught in the building were coming down ladders or leaping into the snow beneath the windows.

What saved a lot of lives was that the House was practically deserted. The main speaker that evening was a man from New Brunswick called Loggie, and he was speaking on fish. So the House was absolutely barren, and Mr. Loggie was alone in his glory.

The Prime Minister, Sir Robert Borden, made his way hatless though the crowd from the Centre Block to his East Block office, where he watched from a window. Dr. Michael Clark, the Member for Red Deer, came reeling out into the snow, gasping and choking. Pierre Blondin, the Minister of State, and Dr. J. D. Reid, the Minister of Customs, brought out Martin Burrell, the Minister of Agriculture, who was badly burned about the face and hands. He had been working in his office next to the reading room where the fire started.

Dr. Edward L. Cash, the Member for Yorkton, and Mr. Thomas MacNutt, the Member for Saltcoats, Saskatchewan, saved themselves by climbing out a washroom window. Robert Rogers, Minister of Public Works, made his way out of the Chamber and down the main corridor in smoke so thick he couldn't see his hand in front of his face. Journalists were holding a ladder for John Stanfield, the Conservative Party whip, to descend from a second-floor window. Madame Sévigny, wife of Albert Sévigny, the Speaker, was rescued through a window in her husband's office. Two of her companions, Madame Bray and Madame Morin, died. Madame Dussault, another of Madame Sévigny's guests, saved herself by jumping from a window. Five others were lost.

Fortunately, the aging Laurier was not in the House that night and was spared the holocaust. A number of famous paintings were destroyed, including the representation by Robert Harris of the Fathers of Confederation at Charlottetown.

When Sam Hughes saw the state of affairs, he summoned the 77th Battalion to aid the City of Ottawa firefighters and the government police. The Corps of Engineers, under Colonel Street, cordoned off the buildings to keep back the huge crowd. The fire had begun at nine o'clock. By eleven o'clock when the Governor General, the Duke of Connaught, arrived with his party from a performance at the Russell Theatre, the fire was at its height, flinging a rippling curtain of flame hundreds of feet over the river.

Sparks rained on the snow-covered roof of the East Block; water from the hoses ran down in rivulets and froze in long, curling streamers. In the East Block were the Prime Minister's office and the offices of the Minister of Justice, the Minister of Finance, the Treasury Board, and the Governor General. Several members reported loud explosions when the fire began, and this no doubt helped to explain the cries of sabotage which immediately arose. The stories which came to the surface of mysterious foreigners, presumably Germans, around the building prior to the fire must be put down to wartime hysteria.

At three in the morning Sir Sam Hughes reported the fire finally under control. The Parliamentary Library alone had escaped undamaged. The government held a midnight Cabinet meeting in the Château Laurier suite of the Minister of Justice,

C. J. Doherty. It was decided there would be no interruptions in parliamentary sittings. After casting about for other quarters the government settled on the Victoria Museum, a gaunt Gothic structure built on a swamp on Argyle Avenue in Ottawa.

I became an editorial writer by attacking one of P. D. Ross's editorials in a letter to the paper. I complained that an editorial he wrote on the constitution was all wind and no sail. This tickled him and he told me to try my hand and see if I could do any better. Thus I began forty years of writing editorials for the same newspaper.

An editorial, a final editorial, was like a Cabinet decision. It represented the considered thinking of the paper. We didn't always agree. We used to meet, the editorial-page staff, P. D. Ross, E. Norman Smith, and myself, and argue like hell. You didn't always get your own way; nor, for that matter, did anyone else.

Once, in an editorial meeting, P. D. stated in an aside that O'Leary didn't belong in Canada; my place was in Tammany Hall with the other Irish. It was all good, clean fun. P. D. gave a dinner for the great Irish journalist T. P. O'Connor, "Tay Pay", when he was in Ottawa gathering money for the cause of Ireland. Outstanding as a journalist and parliamentarian, he wrote for the London *Daily Telegraph* and the New York *Herald* before launching himself in politics on the side of Ireland. When he came to Canada in 1918, I interviewed him at the old Russell Hotel. He had an early-vintage portable typewriter always at his bedside. He was in the habit of waking in the middle of the night and dashing off a page or two of prose, or a few thousand words of speech.

P. D. Ross, tall, spare, a noted oarsman in his youth, with a devotion to the interests of those he liked to describe as "the common crowd", lives on as one of the last great exponents of personal journalism, a newspaperman's newspaperman. P. D. flourished before newspaper offices were taken over by accountants and businessmen with an eye to balance sheets and profit statements. He was aware of these things, but they were secondary. He was interested in news, the inalienable right of people to know; he believed in strong convictions strongly expressed.

He once covered a speech by Macdonald when John A. was so

drunk P. D. couldn't make out his words. He went round next morning to see the Prime Minister and John A. graciously consented to do a re-run of the speech for him. P. D. finished taking notes and, thanking him profusely, rose to go. "Just a moment, young man." Sir John A. gave him a severe look. "I hope this will be a lesson. After this I advise you to refrain from drinking when you are covering an important political meeting."

Once you gained P. D. Ross's confidence he was willing to allow free rein to a person he considered a competent journalist.

E. Norman Smith, who brought the old *Ottawa Free Press* into amalgamation with the *Journal*, and with P. D. became a major architect of the paper's fortunes for over forty years, was of the same ilk.

In October 1927 the Supreme Court of Canada was deadlocked on a petition from the separate school boards of Tiny Township, who were seeking the right to establish Roman Catholic high schools. I knew that P. D. was interested in the outcome and that his views probably would not jibe with mine.

"What do you want me to do?" I asked.

"You write whatever you think is sensible," P. D. said simply, and went off to Florida on vacation. That was his way.

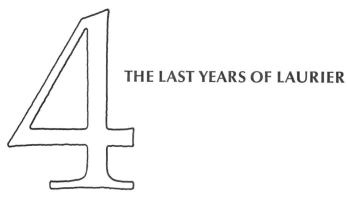

THE LAST YEARS OF LAURIER

My interest in politics sprang to lively caring in the nation's capital. I had arrived in Ottawa at the beginning of one of those periodic convulsions which was to result in the overturning of a Liberal government hoary with fifteen years of office and in the putting into power of a Prime Minister whose position in his own party when the election began was none too secure. Borden and Laurier were the Titans of the day: Laurier marching with grace and dignity into the sunset; Borden, with increasing mastery, making ready to seize the helm.

Louis Riel's hanging in 1885 had launched Laurier as a national figure: his speech on that issue at one bound ranked him among the nation's foremost speakers. In bowing to Orange Ontario pressure Macdonald had committed an egregious political error which was to haunt the Conservative Party for years to come and begin the alienation of Quebec. At his trial, as was clearly revealed in Nicholas Flood Davin's reports, Riel was in the grip of classic schizophrenia, even to hearing voices. Macdonald's statement that Riel should hang "even if all the dogs in Quebec barked" was not calculated to soothe the province's wounded feelings.

Laurier's stand clinched the loyalty of Quebec for himself and his successors, while Macdonald counted on the curés and people like Adolphe Chapleau. They couldn't save him. It was simply a case of blood being thicker than water.

Not long ago I went to see the play *Riel* at the National Arts Centre in Ottawa. At the end of the performance the crowd, ninety per cent English-speaking, rose and cheered Riel to the echo. They were cheering because, after three-quarters of a century, justice was being done.

Of Laurier's speech on Riel the great Edward Blake said, "He had already conquered us in his language, now he's done it in our own." P. D. Ross described it as the noblest speech he ever heard from human lips. Sir Thomas White expressed pride at being able to sit in the same House with a speaker of Laurier's calibre. Of such are history's moments.

Excitement in 1911 centred on the great Reciprocity election. Sir Wilfrid, Prime Minister for fifteen years, was defeated on the issue, viewed by many Canadians as a rejection of ties with the mother country. His stand in favour of an independent Canadian navy had hurt him in English Canada; his earlier refusal to intervene in the abolition of Catholic schools in Manitoba had done him great harm in Quebec. There Laurier faced an implacable alliance of ultramontane clericalists and rabid nationalists under the spell-binding leadership of Henri Bourassa, grandson of Louis-Joseph Papineau.

Negotiated by Laurier and Fielding with the United States, the Reciprocity agreement was a kind of forerunner of the Common Market. It called for breaking down the tariff barriers between the two countries. Opposition to the scheme was based on the fear that commercial union would lead to political absorption. Sir Clifford Sifton bolted the Liberals on the issue, and a slogan made its appearance, "No truck nor trade with the Yankees", not completely strange-sounding to modern ears.

Borden mounted a strong campaign, aided by dissident Liberals, and won the election; the Conservatives took 133 seats to the Liberals' 86. The bad guess on Reciprocity sent Wilfrid Laurier into opposition, there to remain while war broke over Europe.

The burden of conducting the war effort fell on the Conservative Prime Minister, Sir Robert Borden, first, with the introduction of conscription, and second, with the management of the Union Government. Borden took on his task with stern enthusiasm, aided by a young man of glacial calm and sparkling intellect, Arthur Meighen, the Member from Portage la Prairie. To him Borden confided the sharpest and most difficult tasks of his ministry.

Borden had made his reputation before the Supreme Court of

Canada. When he came into the House he was already fully matured and a reservoir of much experience. I heard him speak many times; he spoke without a note, with the mastery that comes only from personal study and not from the prepared effusions of public-relations advisors.

Borden was backed by an aggregation of formidable debaters, Arthur Meighen, R. B. Bennett, F. D. Monk, Thomas Chase Casgrain, to name a few. Laurier, in addition to Pugsley, Charlie Murphy, Michael Clark, and Hugh Guthrie (who later joined Borden's Union Government), had speakers like Jacques Bureau, Ernest Lapointe, and Rodolphe Lemieux, whose fiery debates with the great Quebec nationalist Henri Bourassa drew enormous crowds.

When Borden, Meighen, Laurier, or even Bennett spoke, the ideas and even the words were largely their own; the idea of producing a canned version of events, prepared in a bureaucratic *cul-de-sac* or by some consultant or P.R. adviser, would have been anathema. Men like Thomas Chase Casgrain, Louis T. Pelletier, F. D. Monk were giants in the House, their views carefully thought out, enunciated with skill and verve. They made Parliament work as it was intended to work and no bureaucrat could stand up to them.

There were no P.R. men, no second-guessers, no poll-takers. Members had to get out and find what their constituents were thinking; government had to operate on conviction and principle, not on what the next poll would bring. When Borden decided conscription was necessary if Canada was to continue to make a valid contribution to the defence of freedom, there was only one man he could call on to do the job and that man was Arthur Meighen.

Born in Perth County, Ontario, in 1874 Meighen was elected in Portage la Prairie, Manitoba, in 1908. By 1913 he occupied the relatively undistinguished post of Solicitor General in the Borden government. The post was not a reflection of his standing in the government, for Meighen more than any minister enjoyed the confidence and friendship of Sir Robert Borden.

It was perhaps another example of the inevitability of paradox in politics, the curious fellow-feeling between the aloof, sometimes grim Halifax lawyer and the glacial, superbly brilliant country lawyer from Portage la Prairie. As for the Liberals, they detested Meighen for his ability in the House, for his cool arrogance, for his absolute mastery of issues, and for his refusal to indulge in demagoguery and political quackery. In England Meighen would have stood out by his talents; in the somewhat stultified atmosphere of the Canadian Parliament he was an anomaly, a changeling, almost a political mutant.

Meighen's use of closure to put conscription through made him anathema in the Province of Quebec for the duration of his political life; there is no question he knew precisely the effect that piloting the measure would have on his career; there is no question he thought it was his duty to carry on regardless.

English-speaking Canadians couldn't understand how, when everything they cherished was being menaced, French Canada preferred to remain aloof. It was an attitude all the more difficult to come to terms with in light of the fact that France herself was fighting for her life. The problem was, of course, that English-speaking Canadians couldn't seem to get it through their heads that French Canada, Quebec, didn't give a tinker's curse for France or anything in it. What had France done for them? For two hundred years France had turned its back on French Canada; and now this people, these French Canadians, were concerned only with working their land, populating their province, and looking after their own affairs. Curiously when France, in the person of Charles de Gaulle, appeared at her gates after two centuries of silence, Quebec responded.

Borden, the Halifax lawyer, descendant of United Empire Loyalists, took his party from misty-eyed colonialism to robust Canadian nationalism. His wartime contribution was to maintain the nation intact, keep up the flow of Canadian troops to Britain, put military service on a national basis, and enlist the co-operation of patriotic and sincere men in both major parties to ensure active prosecution of the war effort.

At all times he took a strong position for Canada and Canada's rights. While in London for meetings of the Imperial War Cabinet Borden could level an accusing finger at Lloyd George and, his voice brimming with passion, state that never again would Canadians tolerate a repetition of the blood and horror of Passchendaele, where so many gave up their lives as a monument to British bungling.

Borden did not endear himself to the British imperialists when he insisted that Canada be a separate signatory of the Versailles Treaty. It was Borden who, with Jan Christiaan Smuts, prepared the way for the Statute of Westminster, demanding for Canada and the other dominions what is now accepted as the very es ience of the Commonwealth: full recognition as autonomous nations with complete powers of self-government. He also demanded a voice in foreign policy, consultation in matters of common concern, concerted action founded on consultation. Borden's real legacy was a kind of enlightened nationalism which changed not only the constitutional structure of Canada but the shape of the Empire itself. After Borden, the Empire was on the way out and the Commonwealth on the way in.

Behind the façade that everyone knew — that of the stern, prosaic Halifax lawyer, little acclaimed by his contemporaries, grudgingly acknowledged by history—there was another Borden, a civilized, even sensitive man who could be deeply touched by the poetry of the sunset over the towers and cupolas of the West Block. For seventeen years after his retirement he continued to live in Ottawa at his graceful home, "Glensmere", on Wurtemburg Street, recently demolished to permit construction of a high-rise apartment building.

After the 1917 election I heard reports that Laurier was stepping down. Everybody remembered he had offered his resignation to the caucus in 1915 at the height of the agitation over Ontario's Regulation 17, which restricted the use of French in the schools of that province. When the caucus turned down Lapointe's resolution supporting French language demands, it took the united efforts of the Ontario members to prevent Laurier from quitting.

If the 1915 rejection of Lapointe's resolution was an affront to

Laurier's leadership, the Union Government was, of course, even more destructive. While Borden failed to persuade Sir Lomer Gouin or Rodolphe Lemieux to join him, he did manage to obtain Hugh Guthrie, a former Laurier minister, and western Liberals like James A. Calder, Arthur Sifton, and T. A. Crerar. Sir Clifford Sifton, a mighty voice of Liberalism on the Prairies and owner of the *Manitoba Free Press*, had worked hard to bring about the Union Government.

One of the strange stories of the period is that Mackenzie King, Laurier's defeated Minister of Labour, sent word from the United States, where he was helping the Rockefellers solve their labour problems, that he would be available to serve in a Union Government. Borden didn't want him.

The Union Government won the 1917 election and Laurier took only twenty seats outside Quebec.* I went to see him to try to pin down the rumour that he was planning to resign. I didn't have a great deal of faith in the rumour because in those days leaders didn't resign on account of a simple defeat or two; they were selected to lead in fair weather or foul, in power and out of power, until such time as they were ready to surrender their mandate. Defeat was not a disgrace or a disaster but part of the game.

I found Laurier stretched out on a couch in his temporary office in the Victoria Museum, strangely at home amid the artifacts and curios and reading a life of the Empress of China, to all appearances completely relaxed and oblivious to the currents of rumour and gossip swirling round his leadership. He was not, however, in a mood to reveal secrets.

"I regret, O'Leary, I cannot tell you anything. As a former newspaperman myself, I understand your desire to have information, but you realize if I have anything to say it must be to my party and to the House."

This was, of course, long before that pernicious institution, the press conference, was invented. When a prime minister had something important to say, he said it in the House of Commons. The idea of bringing together a group of journalists in order to deliver

*(1917) Unionist 153, Laurier Liberals 82.

soporific inanities for the afternoon papers was unheard of.

From the war Laurier never recovered politically. He did the best he could, remaining faithful to his Quebec supporters, watching support in the rest of Canada fade to twenty seats in 1917. In holding his Quebec followers he lost support in the rest of Canada. He had a strong hold on English as well as French Canadians, particularly on the Scots in Ontario, who had for Laurier what amounted almost to reverence. One of his favourite gambits while addressing a large audience of Scots was to say that if he hadn't been born French-Canadian he'd have liked nothing better than to be Scots. And they believed him. His charm and sweetness of personality were in sharp contrast to Borden's granitic exterior.

In the seven years during which I reported Laurier in the House of Commons I never heard him speak in French. The reason was simple. He took the attitude that politics was the art of communication. If the majority in the country had spoken Hottentot, Laurier would have mastered Hottentot. His English was faultless, and in his grasp of every shade and nuance of both languages he was without a rival.

Ernest Lapointe arrived in Parliament in 1904, a veritable habitant. Faced with the choice of speaking in French and remaining largely out of the mainstream or learning English, he, too, mastered English. There was nothing in these men of separatism. They would vigorously have repelled any such suggestion. They, like Cartier, were Canadians first, ready to compete on equal terms with English-language Canadians; they had confidence in themselves and their capacity to survive.

Lapointe sought the advice of a compatriot from Three Rivers, Jacques Bureau, whose later involvement in the Customs scandal was to be one of the factors in bringing down King's government in 1926. Bureau bluntly told Lapointe: "If you want to make a name for yourself, you must speak in English."

Lapointe definitely wanted to make a name for himself. The problem has been resolved in our day by simultaneous translation: a member speaks in his language of preference and within seconds his words are translated and electronically conveyed to the ears of his listeners. This facility did not exist in Lapointe's day.

29

Like other great parliamentarians, he almost lived in the Parliamentary Library, that finishing school for so many young M.P.'s. His interventions in the House were marked with the authority which comes from thorough study. In later years, as Mackenzie King's right hand in Quebec (he called King "Rex"), he became French Canada's most influential, most respected representative at the federal level.

Lapointe's appearance was in his favour: erect, dignified, with a commanding voice, he first impressed himself on the party at the 1919 leadership convention when King assumed the mantle of Laurier. It should be noted that when this happened Lapointe had sat in Parliament for fifteen years. Before television, leaders took time to gain experience and maturity. Now, by the magic of the media they are created overnight and vanish as quickly.

Laurier remained in harness until his death early in 1919. As long as his party needed him and he was able by his presence to contribute to national unity, there was no thought of taking up retirement, however welcome. There is no question that but for the great respect in which Laurier was held in his province the nationalist element under Bourassa would have gotten out of hand.

With the possible exception of Macdonald, Laurier remains the greatest of our prime ministers. Striking in appearance, a master of the soft answer, perfectly at home in both languages, he exemplified the best type of Canadianism.

No one in my experience has touched him as an orator: he was the greatest I was privileged to hear in sixty years of observing Parliament. Samuel Butler wrote of Bacon, "Men feared he would make an end." Such was the feeling when Laurier spoke. Enchanted, mesmerized, the silent House gathered unto itself the incomparable wizardry of his words. Mastery of language of course; depth of feeling and passion unrivalled; but more than anything the essence of the man shining through: Laurier's inner greatness inspired people to go with him. When Laurier spoke it was like a first night. Parliament is as quick to appreciate greatness as it is to turn away from the dull pretensions of mediocrity.

Anything but a dry intellectual, he had a thorough sense of

literature and familiarity with history. The House of Commons was his theatre; a theatre in which he remained the leading player. He was a builder, not a destroyer; a unifier, not a sower of discord and division. The ambitions, the desires, even the recreation sought by others in other ways were for Laurier attainable only in the heady passion of parliamentary life.

I remember one of his last appearances, in St. Patrick's Hall in Ottawa, with Lady Laurier, half-blind, tapping the floor with her stick as he spoke. In London, Ontario, I heard his last will and testament to the Young Liberals of Ontario.

. . . remember that faith is better than doubt and love is better than hate. . . .

Such his creed. He was, as Goldwin Smith said of Gladstone, "in the best sense a man of the people; and the heart of the people seldom failed to respond. . . ." Of Lincoln's passing, Walt Whitman wrote that it was as if a giant cedar crashed on a hillside, leaving a lonely place against the sky. So, with the going of Laurier, all of us knew a great light had gone from public life.

When it was time for the House to pay its tribute, Dr. Michael Clark, who had had a bitter falling out with Laurier over conscription, rose to recall that when his son fell in France he received from the Liberal leader a letter noble and touching in its sympathy.

I was one who stood at the graveside as Sir Wilfrid's body was committed to earth following a procession through Ottawa streets in which fifty thousand people took part. I wrote in the *Journal*:

In days gone by Ottawa had seen many vast assemblages but nothing to equal this. All day Friday every incoming train brought its quota of mourners, men and women who had followed Laurier through life and desired to follow his body on its last journey on earth. Far into the night and into the small hours of the morning they stood in line braving snow and cold so that they might look upon the face of the dead knight and when at last dawn came and the doors of the Death Chamber were closed hundreds more were gathering, pleading with

31

the officers who stood guard outside that they be not denied the privilege of a last look at the nation's Grand Old Man. And when finally the doors of the building opened and they were bringing the casket, carried reverently, almost tenderly to the funeral chariot, the place for miles in the vicinity was one blackened mass of humanity. Sir Wilfrid in his mightiest days had made many triumphal marches through the capital's streets, but none so mighty as this.

5 TWO NEW LEADERS

The Liberal Party Convention in 1919, when Mackenzie King, fresh from his wartime sojourn in the United States, replaced the great Sir Wilfrid Laurier, was a watershed for both the Liberal and the Conservative parties. For the Liberals it meant new orientations as King ruthlessly borrowed platforms from the Progressives and later from the socialistic and welfare-slanted C.C.F. As for the Conservatives, their hour of wartime grandeur waning, the Union Government was losing the support of its Liberal elements; Sir Robert Borden, tired and aging, was ready to sit in the sunshine and leave the management of affairs to others.

The 1919 convention was an early revelation of the capacity of the Liberal Party for self-regeneration. In selecting a leader for purely political considerations, it dispensed with the altruistic and heady baggage of noble sentiment with which Conservative gatherings were encumbered. The party owed nothing to King. He had spent the war in the United States working for the Rockefellers, putting together a kind of company union in Colorado, where the miners toiled in abject conditions. The relationship stood him in good stead in later years when preservation of his books and records was made possible by the Rockefeller fortune in the foundation established to perpetuate Laurier House as his deeded gift to the nation.

Nominated at the convention were King; W. S. Fielding, Laurier's Minister of Finance, now seventy-one; George P. Graham; D. D. McKenzie, temporary House Leader; and Alexander Smith, Laurier's organizer and party manager. In his favour King had relative youth (he was forty-four), the fact that he had stood against conscription in 1917, which brought Quebec support, and his skilful if unscrupulous public assumption of Laurier's mantle without waiting for the verdict of the convention.

King, with his utopian idealism and his academic background as author of *Industry and Humanity*—a book which more Canadians have failed to read than almost any other—appeared out of place amid hard-nosed party managers, few of whom had any socialist leanings; that was something for outlandish countries and long-haired people with foreign names. For men like Charles Murphy, Andrew Haydon, Jacques Bureau, Ernest Lapointe, politics was a matter of earthy realism. Socialism had no place in their political spectrum.

A contemporary writer had this description: "It was as though Captain Kidd sailed up the Rideau Canal and his crew were out on shore leave." Well, the party managers were not quite that tough; but there were few dreamers among them. Of the platform produced at the convention, Fielding wrote later: "Like the platform of a railway coach, it was made to get in on."

As he was able to do on several other occasions in his life, King, normally unspectacular, undramatic, more than a little prosy, managed to rise to the occasion with a speech which conciliated his enemies and strengthened his friends.

It was at the 1919 convention that Lapointe uttered his classic definitions of Liberalism and Toryism, definitions cherished in the Liberal Party to this day. "A Liberal is a Liberal because he likes something or somebody; a Tory is a Tory because he hates somebody or something." It was at this convention that Lapointe, with his large frame and powerful voice, established himself as a person of importance in the party and began that public allegiance to King which was to be the dominating characteristic of his political career. He had a knack for getting off statements which stayed in the minds of his listeners; and along with it a power of winning over his adversaries. J. W. Dafoe was a case in point. As editor of the *Manitoba Free Press*, bitter about French Canada's attitude in the war, he at first disliked, then came to understand and admire, Lapointe's essential Canadianism. In the end, Lapointe became one of his heroes.

Dafoe wielded enormous influence in western Canada and his blessing was enough to put Lapointe across, or at least to make him acceptable. Lapointe was in many ways one of the most powerful men we have had, rising to the top echelon but denied the prime-ministership through the accident of being French-Canadian, but even more through his maturing at a time when King was a dominating and self-perpetuating force in his party.

The French debaters came to the fore after the war; Laurier had them but he didn't need them; he was enough. When King took over, Lapointe, Cardin, Cannon emerged as major figures. But things were never the same after the war. Conscription and Regulation 17 did something to mar the spirit between English- and French-speaking Canadians. Before the war, we used to go down to the basement of the House, a room we called the Ark, and sing songs. There was also some drinking. French and English sang the old chansons and everyone got along. The First World War replaced comradeship with a bitter legacy.

When I came to the Press Gallery the rule against Members of Parliament reading speeches was strictly enforced. Men like Laurier, Borden, Meighen, Bennett, King put on virtuoso performances with only a few notes to assist them. A member who rose in his place and read a speech through from beginning to end would have been quarantined. As time went on, speech writers appeared. Radio was coming in and political figures needed help to cope with the unfamiliar medium.

The rule against reading speeches altered when budget speeches became an accepted part of House procedure. It gave an enormous sense of occasion to Budget Night when W. S. Fielding came in with a red dispatch box from which he proceeded to produce, one after the other in perfect sequence, the sections of his carefully structured Budget Address. This lengthy disquisition on the nation's finances was followed immediately by a reply as lengthy and as impressively delivered by Sir George Foster.

But it was also a time of ringing hyperbole in political orations. In one of the early Reciprocity meetings in Glengarry County a speaker elaborated as follows:

If the heavens were a blackboard and the Rocky Mountains were chalk, even then no man could write the fullfillment of this nation's future.

One who campaigned with a certain panache, Charles Murphy, Secretary of State in Laurier's Cabinet, chose to descend on the electors of Russell County by yacht. The craft belonged to Senator Edwards of the lumber family who built 24 Sussex Drive, now the Prime Minister's residence. I was aboard the yacht as it wended a stately progress on the majestic bosom of the Ottawa as far as Rockland, where a giant rally took place. The contrast between the opulence of the yacht and its amenities and the ragged poverty of the village, the general air of hopelessness of the mill employees, was very marked. The right to exploit was regarded as one of the imperishable freedoms.

It was a different House then. It was a time when the political-science schools hadn't contributed their quota of clichés. People spoke as they felt; there was more openness. Speakers didn't have an eye on the all-seeing television screen or the latest opinion poll.

In this environment Arthur Meighen towered like some lonely giant of the forest. Borden gave him the toughest assignments and he took them on without question: conscription, the Wartime Elections Act, the Canadian Northern Railway. In each case Meighen emerged as the strong right arm of the Prime Minister and by his adroitness, ability as an orator, and cool, calm approach to the most emotion-charged issues, earned the respect of his friends and the undying hostility of his political enemies.

Successively Solicitor General, Secretary of State, Minister of the Interior, and Minister of Mines, Meighen went to England with Borden in 1918 to attend the Imperial War Conference. Because Meighen went to Winnipeg in 1919 as acting Minister of Justice to view the effects of the Winnipeg General Strike at first hand, he was indicted as the person responsible for the stern measures taken by the Borden government to restore order, including the arrest of the strike leaders. There was some truth in the suggestion, since Meighen supported the government at every step of the way; his was the most effective and telling voice on the government side; yet it was not accurate to use his position, as his enemies did, in order to discredit him as being anti-labour. He stood for order and good government, and if this in certain circumstances meant being labelled anti-labour, then Meighen was prepared to be so labelled.

His piloting of conscription through the Chamber with the use of closure had earned the undying rejection of Quebec, and his resolutions providing finance for the Canadian Northern and its shifty promoters, Mackenzie and Mann, resulted in lining him up, in the eyes of some, with the railway promoters. R. B. Bennett, whose C.P.R. allegiance made him unalterably opposed to any assistance to the Canadian Northern, went so far as to charge Meighen with being the "gramophone" of Mackenzie and Mann, a delicious tidbit for the Liberal speakers.

Arthur Meighen was named to succeed Sir Robert Borden as Prime Minister of Canada and Secretary of State for External Affairs on July 10, 1920. Meighen was picked by Borden as a result of a poll of the caucus.

The Cabinet's choice had been Sir Thomas White, Borden's Minister of Finance, a party wheelhorse but not a leader. He had been a Liberal but left Laurier over Reciprocity. Transmigration between parties was not in those days viewed with disdain: politicians were allowed the courage of their convictions. White was an imposing figure, pompous, ponderous and pontificating. He had sense enough to say he wouldn't accept the leadership. Some of those who were against Meighen for one and another reason — Ballantyne, Doherty, Calder—wrote a memo to Borden pointing out that Meighen was anathema in Quebec because of his connection with conscription.

Most of Borden's Cabinet was against Meighen: they suspected his brittle toughness, which was based on principle and conviction, not on party advantage; most of them couldn't see the difference. In picking Meighen, Borden felt he was making the right choice, although many thought he was taking a dangerous risk. The backbenchers wanted Meighen. He was incomparably the finest parliamentary mind in the party, the outstanding man in the House. In those days that counted. The House was where the action was.

His record of loyalty to the Prime Minister was second to none.

He had carried through to unflinching conclusion the most unrewarding jobs. These things he had done out of loyalty to his leader and because he believed they were necessary. He deflected a good deal of the lightning from Borden, a political dividend appreciated by the leader. But as a result he suffered political wounds.

It was my fortune to know Arthur Meighen; to know him better, probably, than nearly any other knew him. I admired his mastery of complexities; his probity, his determination to stand by his friends. I knew the other Arthur Meighen, the Arthur Meighen the world seldom saw: firm friend, indulgent father, classical scholar without peer among Canada's parliamentarians.

In 1912 I wrote a piece about Arthur Meighen for the old *Canadian Magazine*, "The White Hope of the Conservative Party". (At that time there was a lot of nonsense talked in boxing about finding a "white hope" — a white man to stand up to the black champion, Jack Johnson.) Meighen liked the piece and congratulated me on it one day when I ran into him in the parliamentary reading room. It was the beginning of a friendship which went on until the day of his death.

Shortly after Meighen became Prime Minister I wrote a piece for *Maclean's* magazine, in which I took the Conservative Party to task on a number of issues. I suggested the party was becoming divorced from its own supporters. I had been invited to attend a dinner celebrating Meighen's leadership at the Country Club in Ottawa. But after my article appeared I was cold-shouldered by so many Conservatives I felt it would be better, less embarrassing for Meighen, if I didn't show up at the dinner.

A day or two before, he called me and said he wanted to be sure I was going to the dinner. I said I wasn't and explained why. He insisted I show up, so to please him I agreed and took my place on the night in question at a table somewhere around the middle of the room in a not-too-conspicuous position. When Meighen arrived he spotted me, came down to my table, and brought me up with him to the head table, where he sat me at his right hand. That was the kind of man Arthur Meighen was.

Some of the big men in the party were jealous of him, among them R. B. Bennett. In comparison with Meighen, Bennett was all bluff and bounce. He was a powerful speaker, his speed of delivery in the House so rapid that he was known as Richard "Bonfire" Bennett.

Bennett made his reputation and most of his large fortune (whatever wasn't left to him by Mrs. Eddy, his childhood sweetheart) as counsel for the c.p.r. in western Canada. He felt this entitled him to special recognition. I once described Bennett as "a competent corporation lawyer with a touch of Moody and Sankey". Another time I said he was "a cross between a hard-nosed corporation lawyer and a political Savonarola". I said he was "rich, purse-proud, and puritanical".

There was something about Bennett which brought out the vitriol in one's pen. I was a little kinder to him on the eve of the 1930 general election. For *Maclean's* magazine I wrote:

> Cradled by the sea, school teacher, lawyer, business man, and
> politician, R. B. Bennett's background will serve him well on the
> bridge of the ship of state.

This was Bennett: prickly, puffed up, and overbearing, he never bothered to hide his jealousy of Meighen, who surpassed him in so many of the things that touched Bennett's pride. At times, though, Bennett was capable of surprising and even endearing touches of frankness. "I'd give anything," he told me one day, "to have Meighen's mind."

Of that there was no chance. One was a bright blade, quick to lop off the head of a foe, splendid in attack or defence; the other a two-handed claymore, swishing in all directions at the same time.

When it came to debating, Meighen had no peer. Even though modern experts, graduates of political-science classes who have never seen the fate of a government hanging on a single word, say that speech-making no longer matters, it just isn't so. In a parliamentary democracy the art of speech-making will always be the primary art. The art of a Churchill, a Roosevelt, a John F. Kennedy. Democracies operate by persuasion, and men are persuaded by ideas and ideas are packaged in words. One of the problems in our time is that we suffer from a paucity of ideas surrounded by a plethora of words.

There was magic in Meighen's brilliant, crystal speeches, carefully structured to a climax, spoken without a single note. To see his mind playing over the most abstruse and complex of subjects, lighting up the dark places, throwing into relief the salient points, illuminating by sheer forensic skill what was dim and incomprehensible, was to watch an artist at work.

Some said he was too mechanical, too clever, too brilliant for the ordinary run-of-the-mill minds of political party supporters; perhaps this was so. Perhaps it is unwise to be clever in politics. Meighen had curious blindnesses; for example his refusal to take Mackenzie King seriously in the controversy with Byng, a refusal which cost him the election. In order to deal with King, Meighen had first to persuade himself that King had a legitimate issue. In spite of everything those of us who were close tried to tell him, he simply refused to take the issue seriously. To do so, he would have had to accept that a majority of Canadians would believe King when he charged the Governor General was both unfair and lacking in frankness. This Meighen could not be persuaded to believe.

Meighen has been called a magnificent failure, arch reactionary, creature of big business, and so on. Each and every one of these derogations was totally false. In one of his first speeches in the House he assailed tariff protection for manufacturers of farm machinery.

He was essentially a very human person. I recall an occasion among many demonstrating this quality. He was to give an address in French. He couldn't find his text, or, curiously, his shirt or dinner jacket or black trousers. I came to his rescue, and the spectacle of Arthur Meighen's lank length perilously encased in my shirt, jacket, and pants was enough to make a saint laugh. Meighen went out with no change in expression, adding to the humour of it, and delivered his remarks in French without a single break. He'd memorized the entire text of some nine or ten pages.

The only time I ever saw him really taken aback was one night when a very witty Jewish Liberal, Sam Jacobs, made a strong protectionist speech, and when he sat down Meighen rose and invited the honourable gentleman to cross the floor and come to his spiritual home. Jacobs got up and said, "Mr. Speaker, one of my ancestors did that sort of thing two thousand years ago, and the world hasn't stopped talking about it yet." Meighen raised his hand in salute.

Once, in a full flow of eloquence in the House, Meighen mentioned a policy he was particularly in favour of. "That's in the platform of the Liberal party," a voice cried from across the floor.

"Mr. Speaker," Meighen shot back, "I am sorry to hear it. Had I a wish dearer to my heart than all others, the worst fate I could fear for it would be that some day it would get into a Liberal platform."

I remember one night when he was speaking the back-benchers on the Liberal side started to boo. Meighen stopped and said, "Mr. Speaker, to an intelligent interruption I have no objection whatever, but I do object, sir, to those ejaculations which ceased to be the language of men ten thousand years ago." You could have heard a pin drop.

WITH MEIGHEN IN LONDON

In 1921 Arthur Meighen as Prime Minister invited me to accompany him to London to a meeting of Empire Prime Ministers. The *Ottawa Journal* was willing and a little flattered so long as I continued to send back regular dispatches. At the same time I was representing *The Times* of London in Ottawa, and the trip gave me the opportunity to call on the editors. I was unable to do so immediately and in a day or so I got a telephone call from the foreign editor, very miffed because I hadn't been around to pay my respects to the "home office" as it were.

He invited me — it was more in the nature of a command performance — to be present at a very formal luncheon attended by half a dozen people, some of them world-famous correspondents, others with titles of nobility, a select company in which I found myself rather abashed. After a couple of cocktails I felt more relaxed, and when they asked me to say a few words about Canada I launched into a violent criticism of England's indifference to the real interests of this country. I gave as an example the slipshod coverage afforded by *The Times* to Canadian affairs. They sat up and took notice.

I dealt with Sir John Willison, Laurier's biographer, publisher of the *Toronto News*, and *The Times* correspondent for Canada. "All he's doing for you," I declared, "is writing for *The Times* what he thinks *The Times* would like to see in *The Times*. All damned nonsense." I raised hell about Britain and the British government and other kindred subjects close to their hearts. Pretty strong stuff but they sat and took it like gentlemen.

Getting back to the hotel I thought, "I've done it now; ruined myself with *The Times*." I was lying on the bed when the phone rang. It was Mr. B. K. Long, Imperial and Foreign Editor. Instead of the expected dismissal he asked me to do a column for next day's paper. They were all greatly taken with my remarks at luncheon. I couldn't believe it.

Meighen saw the column and wanted to know what was going on. Sir John Willison saw it, of course, and mentioned it in a letter now in the Public Archives. He was honest enough to admit there was more than a grain of truth in what I wrote.

One of the people I met on that occasion was Lord Lothian. What interested me about Lothian was that he was in the thick of the negotiations leading up to the signing of the treaty between the British government and the representatives of the Dáil, the Irish Treaty of December 1921. He handled the arrangements to bring Michael Collins, the I.R.A. leader, to London, along with the others. Winston Churchill, as Colonial Secretary, dealt directly with Collins. According to Lord Lothian these two men, both fighters, one a bulldog, the other an Irish wolfhound, hit it off almost immediately. As they were signing, Churchill said, "I may be sacrificing my political career."

"I may," Collins said, "be sacrificing my life."

Collins was killed from ambush on August 22, 1922, and the treaty which he signed in order to bring about peace was disowned by De Valera.

I had lunch with Max Aitken, wearing his new title of Lord Beaverbrook, at his Hyde Park home. Walking in the garden before lunch he asked about the coming elections in Canada.

"I take it Arthur Meighen will win easily." I said Meighen would be defeated. He looked surprised.

"You're his friend, aren't you?"

"That's not what you asked me."

Meighen didn't win the election and I gained a reputation with Beaverbrook as a forthright political prophet.

Although an Ulsterman by descent, Meighen had once taken the chair for Willie Redmond in Canada on a mission to promote Home Rule. Charles Murphy, Laurier's Secretary of State, knew about this and when he heard I was going to London with

Meighen he called me. He had a letter for me to give to T. P. O'Connor, who at this time was putting up a strenuous fight for Home Rule both in the British House and in his newspaper, the London *Star*.

O'Connor was living close to the House of Commons, separated from his wife, a brilliant American girl. As soon as he got my note, to which was attached Murphy's letter, he phoned the hotel and invited me to have lunch. To my astonishment and near panic he had invited some of the giants of the Irish Party: John Dillon, a grand old fighter who succeeded Redmond as leader of the Irish Nationalists; William O'Brien; Joe Devlin, who began in the Canadian House and went to Ireland and was elected there; and several others. They spent the evening asking me questions about Meighen. They wanted to have him to a private dinner with some of the Irish Party at Westminster.

Meighen was delighted; we went down together and there were about a dozen present, all famous fighters for Home Rule and the cause of Ireland, which I had imbibed since childhood. It was such a moment as seldom occurs in the life of an individual. Meighen won all their hearts with his knowledge of Ireland and her history; he had Irish poetry at his fingertips. He told them about D'Arcy McGee and about the Irish in Canada. All in all a wonderful evening—hands across the sea and all that.

I never mentioned the episode in my dispatches. I had a very good reason not to. Meighen was deeply involved at the conference in persuading the British to back out of a treaty of alliance with Japan, which he felt was in the interests of neither Britain nor Canada because of our relationship with the United States, which deeply distrusted Japan's military pretensions. I was thinking of Black Jack Robinson back there in Toronto, editor of the *Telegram*, blaming Meighen for sabotaging the Anglo-Japanese Treaty, doing the work of the Americans to the detriment of Britain, calling him everything short of traitor and looking for something else to pin on him. All he'd need was a story about Meighen hobnobbing with Irish rebels, Sinn Feiners, I.R.A.'s, and the fat would be in the fire.

Since I was with Meighen in a unique position, partly at least as his private secretary, I owed him loyalty. So the story faded quietly away down one of the forgotten corridors of history. Events of twenty years later proved Meighen was dead on in his assessment of Japan's intentions in the Pacific.

A CANDIDATE IN GASPE

In Ottawa Meighen lived in an unpretentious but substantial house on Cooper Street, destined to share the fate of Borden's Sandy Hill home. We were sitting in his den enjoying a chat one day in 1921 when he announced out of a blue sky:

"I'm speaking tomorrow in London, Ontario, and announcing the date of the election."

Well, I was his friend but I was also a reporter, and a hell of a good one if I do say so; and here was the Prime Minister talking about an election.

"I'd like to have the date," I said, "for tomorrow's *Journal*."

He gave me a rather distant look. "I can't do that."

"Suppose I put it in an editorial. You'll be well on your way to London by the time anyone reads it."

I made the proposal in absolute good faith and he accepted it the same way. We both forgot about Canadian Press, which had the right to use our material; somehow a copy of my editorial got over to the Canadian Press office and some enterprising fellow wrote a story and put it on the wire, attributing the announcement of the election to an editorial in the *Ottawa Journal*. Well, of course, the *Globe* picked it up, so when Meighen got off the train in Toronto the following morning, there was a *Globe* headline staring him in the face, announcing the date of the election. He went ahead and made his speech as promised, without any change in the date. Never did he mention the incident to me. That was Arthur Meighen.

As I had predicted to Beaverbrook, Meighen and the Conservatives lost the election, and by a margin greater than even I expected. Meighen was defeated by conscription and Quebec's rejection of him as the Minister who brought it in; even more, he was defeated because of the power of a growing farm movement sweeping the country, a sort of agrarian reaction against the fear and uncertainty of the 1920 post-war recession.

The Conservatives under Meighen went down to 50 seats, compared to 117 for Mackenzie King's Liberals. The second-highest number of seats was held by the Progressive Party, an amalgam of western farm groups under the leadership of T. A. Crerar. In spite of the fact that the Progressives held 64 seats in the Parliament of 1921, Crerar refused to sit as Leader of the Opposition and in the next couple of elections saw his party strength frittered away by desertions to the Liberals. Finally, he joined Mackenzie King's government in 1929, just in time to meet defeat at the hands of R. B. Bennett.

Immediately after the 1921 election King began assiduously courting the Progressives, whom he had energetically attacked during the campaign. With progressive support, King managed to carry on until 1925. In the election of that year, Arthur Meighen campaigned brilliantly against a lack-lustre Mackenzie King. Unfortunately, although a candidate, I was not one of the 116 Conservative members returned with Arthur Meighen.

That election was my baptism in backyard politics, politics at the riding level; such a baptism that it dulled for many years to come the bright edge of any political aspirations I might have had.

I was in Australia when the cable came from Meighen announcing the election for October 29 and calling me home. The reason he cabled me was that in some kind of fit of abstraction or mental aberration I had allowed my name to stand for the riding of Gaspé and, for want of a better Conservative candidate, they had nominated me.

A few weeks after the nomination meeting, P. D. Ross presented himself at my office in the *Journal* and said, "How'd you like to go to Australia?"

I jumped at the offer. I'd never been to Australia. He said, "All right, you're going to go to represent the *Journal* at the Imperial Press Conference."

My wife and I left Vancouver by ship in late July. There were a number of important British press representatives on board, including John Jacob Astor, the proprietor of *The Times,* whose wife was a daughter of Lord Minto, former Governor General of Canada. There was also Lord Burnham, who owned the *Daily Telegraph.* He had all the clichés, "our far-flung Empire" and "our sea-divided race" and so on. In fact, we used to have a pool on him. We would put all these phrases in a bag and pluck them out for ten shillings. If he said "far-flung Empire" first, the holder won. One day Lady Burnham came along and said, "What are you gentlemen doing?" We told her and she said, "I'd like to join in this." She put in her ten shillings and she won the pool, and every day after that when he was speaking, and he spoke every day, tiresome old fellow, she would come and get into the pool.

A. P. Herbert was there, representing *Punch,* Anthony Eden was there for the *Yorkshire Post,* and J. W. Dafoe for the *Manitoba Free Press.* The twenty-one-day voyage gave me an opportunity to compare political notes with Dafoe and I seized the occasion to ask him why he was such a dyed-in-the-wool Grit. "Very simple," he replied. "I simply think of all the sons of bitches in the Tory Party, then I think of all the sons of bitches in the Liberal Party, and I can't help coming to the conclusion that there are more sons of bitches in the Tory Party."

We'd been away a little over a month and were just beginning to enjoy Australia when Meighen's cable arrived. We crossed the Pacific in a ship called the *Tahiti,* and after thirty-five days' travelling I arrived in Gaspé in the middle of a dreadful October snowstorm. Everywhere wires were down and roads were blocked.

Somehow I got to the hotel in Chandler. The proprietor, one of our party organizers, proceeded to introduce me to some of the local chieftains. I was tired and I got away and went up to my room, hoping to get some sleep. Through the paper-thin wall came the sound of voices.

"What do you think of him?" asked a voice.

"Not much to look at," said the other dismally.

"Let's hope he's better than he looks."

"He writes for *Maclean's* magazine," said the other, and I realized they were discussing me.

1. The twinkling eye and cheerful grin.

2,3,4,5. From a series of photographs taken at the *Ottawa Journal* in 1922: (*above left*) Grattan O'Leary, (*right*) Thomas G. Lowrey, Managing Editor, (*opposite page, above*) P. D. Ross, President of the *Journal*, (*below*) his partner and successor as Editor and President, E. Norman Smith.

6 & 7. (*Above*) Robert Borden
and Sir Wilfrid Laurier in 1913.
(*Below*) Arthur Meighen.

8 & 9. (*Opposite page, above*)
G. Howard Ferguson and
R. B. Bennett confer with
J. H. Thomas and Lord Hailsham
at the World Economic
Conference, London, in 1933.
(*Below*) Mackenzie King at
Laurier House.

10 & 11. (*Left*) The one-time apprentice seaman later sailed the Atlantic in comfort on the s.s. *Lady Rodney*. (*Above*) Mrs. O'Leary and daughter Moira about 1932.

12 & 13. (*Opposite page, above*) In press tunic to cover the post-war Potsdam Conference, 1945. (*Below*) With his dog, Timmy.

"I don't give a damn who he writes for. He still doesn't look much like a candidate to me." Rolling over, I consoled myself with the thought that a prophet is without honour in his own country. This was my country and I was obviously not overburdened with honour.

The next morning I said to my friend the hotel man, "Who were the two men in the room next to mine?"

"The president and vice-president of your local organization," he said. My spirits sank, if possible, even lower than they had been.

"By the way," he said, "while you were away in Australia the former candidate spread a rumour that you were ill and not coming back to the riding. He persuaded the members of the association to hold a convention to replace you. They did and they elected him."

"That's fine." I got up from the table.

"Where are you going?"

"Right back to Ottawa. This is the best news I've had since I arrived."

"You can't do that."

"Why not?"

"We've decided to have one more convention to settle the matter."

Reluctantly I agreed. If this was politics I wanted to get back to honest reporting. The convention was held and by some miracle I won. The word had gotten round apparently that I was Meighen's man, and as long as I was official candidate money would be forthcoming. After the meeting my rival came to me and said, "You are Mr. Meighen's great friend. I know he will win the election. I want you to promise me that you will get me a job in Ottawa."

What could I say? With a confidence I was far from feeling I agreed. He said he was going to organize the Magdalen Islands and disappeared. A few days later, Mr. Langlois, my organizer, came to me and said, "Where is the money?"

"What money?"

"The money for the campaign."

Of course, there had to be money to run an election. Stupid of me not to think of it. "Where does the money usually come from?"

Mr. Langlois looked at me pityingly. "You must go to the party headquarters in Montreal."

"Of course. I'll do that right away." I climbed on a train and went to Montreal that afternoon. The party office was on St. James Street where Mr. Patenaude, a former member of Borden's government, was in charge. Patenaude in fact had left Borden over conscription, unlike Albert Sévigny, who stayed with the ship and whose memory on that account is worthy of honour. Patenaude's office was filled with candidates looking for money. He looked rather surprised to see me.

"The money for Gaspé was given out some weeks ago, after the convention."

I said I had been away in Australia and had returned, and I was the official candidate. We made no conjectures as to where the money went, something that was all too obvious. Now I knew why my friend had left for the Magdalen Islands.

Patenaude thought for a moment. Then he brightened. "A very big man in Montreal is coming through with $50,000 for the campaign. I want you to get in touch with him and tell him your problem. If it's all right with him, then it's all right with me."

He gave me the man's name and he was right. He was J. W. McConnell, sugar millionaire and publisher of the *Montreal Star*. He was indeed a big man in Montreal. The only problem was that he was generally known as a Liberal. However, I managed to reach him and he said immediately, "Go back to Gaspé, and when you get there go to the Bank of Toronto."

Following these mysterious instructions to the letter, I arrived in Gaspé on Sunday night and got a room at Baker's Hotel. I asked the proprietor if he knew the manager of the Bank of Toronto.

"A damn Tory like you," was his reply.

Although a cavalier way of treating a paying guest, it was a good augury for the settlement of my financial problems.

I called the bank manager at his home and he said that $4,000 had been deposited to my credit that day. This was reassuring. Somebody cared about the Conservative Party in Gaspé. I made the mistake of calling my organizer, Mr. Langlois, and telling him the news. Next morning when I went to the bank to get the money the entire Conservative organization of Gaspé followed me in. I felt like the Pied Piper. It was the last time they followed me anywhere.

Of course, I hadn't a chance from the beginning. My opponent, the Honourable Rodolphe Lemieux, a tower of strength in the Liberal Party, Speaker of the House of Commons, ran his campaign with a federal ship, the *Lady Grey*, up and down the coast. I was naive enough to denounce this blatant exercise of patronage until a very wise old Conservative, William Flynn (an uncle of Senator Jacques Flynn), pointed out to me that I was helping Lemieux to get re-elected.

"You're making him out a hell of a big man in Ottawa," said Mr. Flynn. I saw the logic and desisted. Well, of course, we had to have the classical encounter dear to Quebec hearts, the "assemblée contradictoire", at which each candidate was allowed an hour to speak. It was an endurance contest, the place packed to the rafters, wreathed in smoke from hand-rolled "Alouette" cigarettes, a situation in which the man with the loudest voice had all the advantage.

I didn't have the loudest voice, but I could make myself heard, and I was confident I could hold my own. Lemieux began with diabolical cleverness by paying high tribute to my career as a Press Gallery man in Ottawa, a young man of promise and brilliance, a credit to Gaspé.

Torn between being puffed up at these amazing and apparently sincere compliments and a suspicion that I was being had, I listened while he went on to express his distress at "coming down here and finding my young friend O'Leary the candidate of the Protestants and Jews". A rumble went round the room at this shot and I denied hotly that I was anyone's candidate except the voters'. The damage was done. I could feel the hostility creeping round me. I got through my remarks in stony silence from the crowd.

"That was a terrible thing to say," I accused Lemieux afterward. "I thought you were a gentleman."

"Don't take it to heart, young man." He laid a friendly hand on

51

my shoulder. "It doesn't matter what we say here. There are no reporters. Chalk it up to experience." Whereupon he invited me to join a dinner party on the government ship. Of course, I refused. I went back to my hotel in a mood of disillusionment. There was more to politics than simply putting up your case and your party's case in the most persuasive way possible. I was beginning to feel like a fly in a web.

Lemieux's brother, an equally able politician, was Minister of Education in Quebec, and before the election there was a long delay in paying teachers' salaries. A week or so before voting day he came down and sat on the platform while Rodolphe Lemieux explained to the hall full of voters that the Minister from Quebec was here tonight and he had brought with him, at the particular request of his brother the federal candidate, the salary cheques for the teachers of Gaspé — which he proceeded to distribute to as many teachers as happened to be present; which was usually quite a few, since everyone who was able to walk went to the political meetings. By the time the election came on the voters began to get the idea Lemieux was a cross between God and Moses. They didn't dare vote against him. Some people think the art of running elections came in with the P.R. boys and the advertising agencies. The organizers of fifty years ago could show them tricks they never heard of.

My last meeting was held in a town called Chandler. The Liberals had packed the hall with, of all things, old ladies, and when I came out on the platform they beat the floor with their canes and cried out in a kind of sing-song chant in French, "Conscription! Conscription! Conscription!" It was unsettling to say the least. The idea was, of course, that Meighen was going to take all their sons and put them in the army to fight Britain's wars. I am sure they firmly believed this. That didn't make it easier for me.

The only place where I won a majority was a town of two thousand called Grande Rivière. Most of Lemieux's relatives lived there. They must have known him pretty well. I was not too discouraged by defeat. As a matter of fact, I felt rather relieved as I returned to Ottawa and the relative sanity of the Parliamentary Press Gallery.

Meanwhile, my friend the former candidate had vanished as though the Magdalen Islands, if such a thing were possible, had opened and swallowed him up. I never gave him a thought until, about six years later, when Bennett was Prime Minister and Arthur Meighen was government leader in the Senate, he walked into my office in the *Ottawa Journal* and demanded the government job I had promised. I made no mention of the missing funds. What was the point? I spoke to Meighen and he was given a job in the Senate and performed well and faithfully for many years.

KING, BYNG, AND MEIGHEN

The Conservative Party under Meighen did a lot better nationally in 1925 than I did in my lonely battle in Gaspé. Meighen came back with 116 members, compared to 101 for Mackenzie King, who was defeated in his own seat, North York. The Progressives went down to 24 seats.* At this point, following any reasonable interpretation of constitutional usage, having had four years to persuade the electors of the validity of his policies and having received a stinging rebuff, King should have gone to the Governor General and tendered his resignation. For Mackenzie King such a course would have been incredibly straightforward and naive. Not one to give up power if any alternative was available, King was determined to hang on until the last ditch.

Of course, Meighen should have insisted that King resign; but Meighen was trapped by his reluctance to interfere with the Governor General's prerogative. Instead of resigning, the farthest thing from his mind, King went to the Governor General and informed him of his intention, as was his right, of meeting Parliament. He also informed him that he expected to secure the necessary backing from the Progressives to maintain control of the House. Thus the first subtle, careful moves leading to the constitutional imbroglio known to history as the "King-Byng Episode". It was more than an episode; it was a situation perilously close to anarchy, and a situation King was to create again

---

*This was a gain of 66 seats for the Conservatives, and a loss of 16 seats for the Liberals and 40 for the Progressives. The number of seats in the House had been increased from 235 to 245.

over the conscription issue fifteen years later. When it came to holding power there were few risks he wasn't prepared to face.

In acknowledging King's right to meet the House, Byng extracted from him the undertaking (in fact King volunteered it) that if he failed to control the House he would gracefully give way and the Governor General should call upon Arthur Meighen and the Conservatives.

At this point it is necessary to advert to the personality and endowments of Julian Hedworth George Byng, first Viscount Byng of Vimy. Bluff, brave, suffering from excessive naivete about politics and politicians, particularly of the Mackenzie King stripe, Byng's distinguished career as a soldier of the Empire had done nothing to prepare him for the kind of deviousness and wiliness exemplified in the lifelong habits of William Lyon Mackenzie King. The very best type of British soldier, Byng was at the same time the very worst type of Governor General, totally incapable of grasping the political intricacies of a country like Canada.

The thought that he might be involving himself in a situation in which he could be made use of to further the political stratagems of the Prime Minister was foreign to his mind—and probably to Meighen's at that moment. And perhaps King himself had not yet fully elaborated the use to which the Monarch's representative would be put in giving him an unshakable grip on power. There were many steps to take, many procedural and political watersheds to be crossed, before King could see his course clear before him. He was moving the pieces quietly, skilfully into place. The first step was to meet Parliament, not as Leader of the Opposition as he should have done, but as Prime Minister. At the same time he had successfully neutralized Meighen, who could not protest without appearing to criticize the Governor General; and this Meighen would not do.

So we have on one side a man of honour playing by the ancient and traditional rules; and on the other a man of overweening ambition, ready to cast aside rules, traditions, even his gentleman's agreement with Byng, to cling to power. The episode was extremely illustrative of the characters of both men: King needed power to bolster his personal inadequacy, the neurosis that drove him to quacks and mediums; Meighen was complete and sufficient unto himself.

With the help of the Progressives King was not doing too badly: he survived a number of non-confidence votes and even got approval for his Budget; in this way he felt, according to his apologists, that he had discharged his undertaking to Byng. He had fulfilled the first condition of controlling the House.

Everyone knew the tenuous situation could not long endure; the ultimate struggle could not be far off. Meighen, trying to recoup his position in Quebec, made what was for him an egregious error. Speaking at Hamilton he committed himself to the principle that Canada should not be drawn into foreign conflict again without a general election.

His reason for taking this stand was purely political. He had come through an election during which in one province he had been labelled an errand boy for Britain, ready to send young Canadians to die in Empire wars. Over Meighen hung the shadow of wartime conscription and the Chanak episode when, after his first defeat by King, he was ill-advised enough to say that Canada must reply "ready, aye, ready" to a request from Lloyd George for help to stop the aggressive Turks at the Dardanelles.

King immediately heaped scorn on Meighen's reversal of his conscription stand. In the event of a crisis the government must accept its responsibilities; Meighen was trying to hide behind the people. And yet, fifteen years later, when King as Prime Minister had to make the decision, he took refuge in a plebiscite, the very thing for which he had scorned Arthur Meighen; and fobbed off his responsibilities with the most insipid phrase in Canadian political history, "Conscription if necessary, but not necessarily conscription."

The cloud that overhung King's government in 1926 was considerably bigger than a man's hand: a cloud which from tiny beginnings grew until it filled the entire political horizon. The Customs Department under King's Minister, Jacques Bureau, Lapointe's old friend, had become riddled with corruption. Customs officials employed to prevent smuggling were actively engaged in catering to the needs of millions of thirsty Americans caught in the grip of prohibition, that curious exercise in mass insanity which gripped the United States after the First World War.

King, of course, claimed the affair was under control; promised full investigation and redress. His first move was the curious one of appointing Jacques Bureau, a jovial and entertaining gentleman, to the Senate. Harry Stevens pounded away at King on the corruption in Customs, documenting his attacks with a mountain of evidence. King managed to get a Select Committee appointed which for the time being deflected the lightning of Stevens's wrath. The committee sat for five months and reported that there was indeed a scandal and that government employees were implicated.

Stevens immediately moved no confidence in the King government. J. S. Woodsworth, an ascetic little man in a goatee, of noble intentions and political naivete, who had nursed distrust of the Conservatives and particularly of Meighen since the Winnipeg strike, attempted to save King by an amendment calling for a Royal Commission, a transparent ploy, having little effect other than to put King's certain defeat off until the weekend. Not even the Progressives were prepared to swallow what had gone on in the Customs Department under Bureau. When Woodsworth's amendment was defeated, King knew the game was up.

For King it was a weekend of scurrying around, of consultations with the living and the dead, of lonely reflections and meditations, of trembling resolve. At last his mind was made up. He would not, could not, face defeat in the House.

On Monday morning the Governor General was confronted in his office by the chubby man with the round, pink face and outthrust, pugnacious jaw, demanding dissolution, a new election. Byng, perturbed, nonplussed, fixed King with his steely, nononsense eyes, the eyes that had gazed on Vimy Ridge: hadn't they made an agreement; wasn't it understood that, failing to control the House, King would hand over the reins to Meighen?

The pudgy little man wasn't having any. With an impatient movement (King could be autocratic in the grip of his convictions) he thrust all that aside, all talk of agreements, of handing over the government to his pale, sneering rival whom he detested. Wasn't that months ago? After all, he was Prime Minister of Canada. Was he expected to remember every little nuance, every gesture of a meeting more than seven months gone?

King's eyes almost filled with tears when he thought of all he had sustained in those months, the want-of-confidence motions, the jibes and taunts of Meighen and his crowd, the horrors of scandal; and now when he had survived all that, had operated his lame-duck government for six long months for the benefit of the country, this red-faced little Britisher was holding him to a casual undertaking, of whose details he could no longer even be certain! Byng was calmly telling him he was no longer prepared to serve his, Mackenzie King's, purpose. As far as Byng was concerned, the agreement covered the full term; and if King was unable to carry on at any time prior to the end of his term, then Meighen had to be given a chance. That was the undertaking.

Fortified by his consultations with the spirits, strong in the knowledge of his dead mother's approval, King wanted an election. When this was rejected, he simply tendered the Governor General his resignation. Not completely aware of the storm he was walking into, that doughty soldier did the only thing left for him to do. He summoned Meighen. When one division falls, throw another one in.

From then on King sat in the House, throwing up his hands, completely out of it, refusing to co-operate in any way. As far as he was concerned, the country was without a government; as in fact it was.

This left Meighen in a position where he could do one of two things, accept or refuse. If he refused, that meant, of course, an election, with no government in office; no one to run the country during the two months prior to the election. It also meant in a sense repudiating Byng, who had made an agreement. This Meighen could not do.

Borden was consulted; Borden said, "You have no choice." There were warning voices. Dr. Beauchesne, the grand old Clerk of the House of Commons, a man of immense prestige, got word to Meighen through R. B. Hanson that politically he was putting himself in King's hands. Meighen was not deterred.

Grit analysts have characterized King's conduct up to this point as diabolically clever, Machiavellian. It may have been; it may have been sheer pique. It was a case of one man being prepared to carry out his responsibilities when the other had thrown in his hand. Meighen has been criticized on tactical grounds. But who better served his country, the man who acted in accordance with his judgment of where his duty lay, or the man who, devious and impenetrable, concentrated his energy on one thing, the seizure of power?

Meighen set himself to the task of government. Unable to appoint ministers who would have had to resign their seats and run again in accordance with existing constitutional provisions, he named acting ministers who were, of course, challenged in the House by King on the grounds that they didn't form a proper government.

Meighen managed to get passage of the censure motion based on the Customs corruption; but there was little point in this since King had resigned. King demanded Meighen's resignation (he indulged in no canting piety about "co-operating" with Meighen in running the country as more recent leaders have been wont to do). King was motivated by one concern: to get back in power as soon as possible. He identified Canada's welfare in the most intense and personal way with his own. Meighen scornfully refused to resign and King brought in a motion challenging the government's right to govern when the ministers had not been confirmed in office. The Progressives saw a wonderful opportunity to rid themselves of Tory bedfellows and voted with the Liberals.

The worst part of Meighen's defeat in the House was that it was purely accidental. A Progressive member called Bird was paired with an absent Conservative called Kennedy. Inadvertently he voted, and the motion was carried by one vote.

There was only one course open to Byng and that was to grant Meighen the dissolution he had refused King. King had his election issue: Byng should have granted him dissolution when he asked for it. He would argue that Byng had turned down the advice of the Monarch's duly constituted first adviser. Whitehall was attempting to dictate to Canada, reducing Canada from Dominion status to that of a Crown colony.

On that issue King fought the election, putting forward a carefully elaborated argument to the effect that Byng, with some kind of mystic connivance with the Tories (perhaps a communication through osmosis or extrasensory perception), had juggled the cards against him. Thus the man who had gone back on his word, the Prime Minister sworn to uphold the constitutional process, was using his own rejection of that process as a bludgeon to batter his way back into office, and in so doing was demeaning the Governor General.

Byng's side of the story has never been told. Servant of the Crown, he kept his lips sealed. Byng had a strong point in his favour in refusing King dissolution and it was this: a government facing a vote of censure cannot ask for and get dissolution as a way of evading the result of the vote. Edward Blake dealt with this very clearly in 1873. And yet King insisted, and Byng could not tell his side of the story.

These things were of small consequence to King. He had an issue that people thought they could understand: interference from Downing Street. A Prime Minister had been told he could not have an election. It offended against the Canadian sporting spirit. Were we to be told when and under what circumstances we were to have national elections?

Meanwhile Meighen, constitutional expert that he was, saw the transparency of King's demagoguery and dismissed it as "froth". It was not froth. It was catching on. This Meighen couldn't believe and, not believing, revealed a chink in his armour, an Achilles heel that King speedily exploited. Meighen knew the constitutional argument was hollow and wouldn't fight it; King knew it appealed to some feeling deep in Canadians who wanted, in a home-grown metaphor, to paddle their own canoe, and pushed it to the full.

Those of us who were in Meighen's confidence became increasingly nervous as King carried his case to the people. I told Meighen, "King is making hay with this." It just didn't register. He went on conducting his own campaign — Empire preference, the economy, the Customs scandal (which King had managed somehow to bury completely in the public mind), protective tariffs—dismissing the Byng issue with a few cutting phrases. He scorned to drag the Governor General into the campaign and

60

thought nearly to the end that Canadians would see through King's shabby ploy.

In western Ontario, where memories of the old Scottish reformers lingered on, King fought as William Lyon Mackenzie's grandson, reviving the old fight against domination by Downing Street. We tried to tell Meighen that King was digging his (Meighen's) grave. I remember Arthur Ford, editor of the *London Free Press*, going repeatedly to Meighen, saying King was making tremendous headway in western Ontario on the constitutional issue. Stubborn, proud, unbending, Meighen sent back his answer, "I am not getting down to that level." He couldn't bring himself to believe the people of Canada were stupid enough to be taken in. Perhaps there is a moral in all this: never overestimate the intelligence of the electorate.

At last, realizing what was happening when it was too late, Meighen spoke in Guelph in a masterly performance, demolishing King's position, showing up the hollowness of it, the sham. In those days there were no radio and television networks to carry news instantly to the public; Meighen's speech was lost in the shuffle. It never got out to the people.

In 1926 King came back with 116 seats to Meighen's 91, picking up 11 seats in Ontario and the rest scattered through the Maritimes.* He carried, of course, his Quebec insurance, 60 seats, a near-guarantee of power regardless of issues, as long as the rest of the country could be fragmented, as he succeeded in doing on the Byng issue. Once again the Quebec Liberal bloc proved a dagger at the heart of Conservative hopes.

Outside Quebec King held only 56 seats compared to 87 for Meighen; the same phenomenon worked for Pearson against Diefenbaker and for Trudeau against Stanfield. On this occasion it meant the end of political aspirations for the man painted with the conscription brush in Quebec.

Of course, conscription was a handy stick to beat a dog with in Meighen's case. The same stick was used against Bennett; he was

---

*(1926) Liberal 116, Conservative 91, Progressive 13, Liberal-Progressive 9, United Farmers of Alberta 11, Others 5. In 1925 the Liberals had taken 101 seats to the Conservatives' 116.

described as "anti-Quebec", while Diefenbaker was going to see that teaching nuns no longer wore habits. Essentially, all this meant simply that block voting as a source of power was too useful and too precious for the managers of the Liberal Party to allow Quebec to go its way. Regardless of leaders and policies, the Liberal Party must go on being the instrument of Quebec's march to power, a principle guaranteeing minority rule in our country.

If you take your history from the Press Gallery or from television you get the impression that Meighen won all the debates and King won all the elections; that simply isn't true. In the case of the 1921 election, that was lost by Borden and the Union Government under the impact of conscription in Quebec. For that Meighen could hardly be blamed; no one else would have done better.

In 1925 Meighen took the Conservatives from 49 seats to 116; the Liberals under King went down from 118 to 101. King himself was defeated with eight of his ministers. That hardly bears up the current and general belief that King was a super-politician. As a matter of fact, even in 1926 the Conservative vote under Meighen exceeded the Liberal vote by 80,000.

To one who has witnessed the events, the reconstruction of history bolstering Liberal Party mythology is unnerving: books by people who were not present describe in detail Mackenzie King's tremendous political skill, his understanding, his determination to maintain unity. Stuff and nonsense. His desire for unity was manifested in encouraging his people in Quebec to keep alive the fires of anti-conscription sentiment. Never were French Canadians to be allowed to forget that it was the Tory Party that put through legislation sending their sons overseas to fight a foreign war. It wasn't the unity of Canada but the unity of the Liberal Party that concerned him.

In order to counteract the Liberal propaganda on conscription, Meighen made his famous statement in Hamilton after the 1925 election. Meighen did not help himself one iota in French Canada and he did himself considerable harm in English Canada.

One of the unforeseen and even tragic by-products of the Hamilton statement was the breaching of the long friendship between Meighen and Tom Blacklock of the Parliamentary Press

Gallery. Tom, Laurier's confidant, was Meighen's close friend. He was frequently privy to Meighen's strategy and plans.

He never got over the Hamilton statement. He felt Meighen had betrayed his own instincts in an attempt to cater to Quebec. Meighen tried to patch things up one night when half a dozen people were gathered for the interminable Wednesday-night poker game. Arthur Meighen came in and Tom got up and went out; Meighen followed him and said, "I want to speak to you." And Tom replied, "I don't want to speak to you. Now or ever." I saw it happen, a direct cut of Arthur Meighen by Tom Blacklock. I know Arthur Meighen was hurt, although he professed immunity from sentiment. "Whatever people may expect of me, they shouldn't expect emotion," he often said.

When Tom Blacklock died quite a few years after, they took him up to Halton in Ontario to bury him; he was pretty much alone, most of his friends and relatives gone. And Arthur Meighen, long past his days as Prime Minister and party leader, turned up at the funeral; he asked permission to speak and delivered a very touching and impressive eulogy on Tom Blacklock.

I was as close to Meighen as anyone outside his family could be. He gave me a bit of advice I have always attempted to follow: "Never have a manuscript of a speech. If you use one once you become a slave to it. Learn to think on your feet, organize your thoughts. For a while you may suffer the pains of hell, but eventually it comes to you." I can say truthfully that I never wrote a line for him. He didn't require it.

His speeches were models of clarity and extemporaneous virtuosity. There was nothing accidental about it: when he rose to speak, the subject, whatever its nature, by long study and meditation was at his fingertips. His speeches on railway questions were masterpieces of exposition. It was Meighen who put together the Canadian National Railways on the basis of the acquisition of the Grand Trunk system. His speech outlining this policy, delivered to the Canadian Club in Montreal in November 1919, lingers in memory. Without a note Meighen held his audience for over an hour on that most difficult of questions, Canadian transportation policy.

He was an authority on D'Arcy McGee; his speech on McGee's hundredth anniversary was a classic. Charles Murphy brought Martin Conboy, president of the American Bar Association. Sir Edward Beatty, president of the C.P.R., was there. It was 1925 and Meighen was Leader of the Opposition; Mackenzie King had to sit and listen to his oratory for nearly an hour, a performance that must have been more than a little distasteful to him. Following Murphy's introduction, Meighen, with a kind of sentimentalism I had never seen him display in public, referred to "the tie that binds Irish hearts".

His great regret in parliamentary life was that he never got to know Laurier really well. But it was his boast that in all the years he had never said one personal word against Laurier. "I found he was too good a man," he said.

I don't think he ever went to sleep without reading a few lines of Macaulay's verse. He kept his mastery of the language honed to a fine edge on the works of the giants of the past. Ideas and language, the marriage between words and ideas: this was Meighen's forte. And to hear Mackenzie King snivelling and whining in his dominie's voice about how he'd been put upon in some way or other, or how destiny hadn't given him his due, or how the Opposition was frustrating his pure-minded effort to impart political salvation; and then the clear, cool rush of Meighen's words like a mountain stream—a study in contrasts!

Meighen was one of those always scaling some mystic Parnassus whose outlines, dimly perceived by others, were crystal clear to his eagle gaze. He shirked no task, however hard or unpopular, in the interest of his country. He was one of those rare people always a little larger than the position they occupy; not a man who could be dominated by power, he rather tended to rise above it.

Nor was he diminished in defeat. As I watched the realization grow that he could not linger longer in politics, I saw no indication of chagrin, recrimination, or bitterness, and in fact you may search his speeches in vain for repining. He was the product of a system where the Opposition role is accorded nearly equal precedence with that of the Government and where defeat no less than victory has its obligations. Certain it is that of Arthur Meighen never could it be said that he struck his flag or besmirched its colours.

When he had made up his mind to go — and it was his own freely taken decision — it was because he felt that, having done what he could for his country, having given unstintedly of himself, and having been rejected on an issue where he felt right was on his side, he now owed something to his growing family.

He launched himself in business and in a few years made a very respectable income, perhaps not quite on a par with Bennett's but certainly nothing to be sneezed at. Financial security achieved, he returned to his love, public affairs, in the Senate, which he adorned with grace and dignity until the Second World War, emerging briefly as interim Conservative Party leader in 1942, only to be defeated in his bid for a seat in York South as a result of an under-the-table bargain between the Liberals and the C.C.F.

Meighen had been granted a tremendous ovation at the Winnipeg convention of the party in 1927. He was also subjected to blistering attack by Howard Ferguson, the Premier of Ontario. Ferguson's speech was completely outshone by Meighen's performance; had Arthur Meighen wished to ask for it he could have had the leadership without difficulty. He had other plans, however, and the leadership went to Richard Bedford Bennett, the New Brunswick boy who had made good in the West as counsel for the C.P.R., Lord Beaverbrook's lifelong friend, and the man who would wrest the prime-ministership from King.

Closing his convention speech Meighen said:

Even here at this Convention the supreme consideration is not who shall be the leader of this party? The supreme consideration is, what manner of party shall he have to lead?

He pleaded for unity and loyalty to the principles of Conservatism, "the flag that floats above us, worthy of those ideals of British liberty and justice which have sent their light forth and their truth among all races of man."

Meighen could rise to heights of eloquence, as in his defence of

Byng in the last speech of the 1926 campaign, delivered at Co-
bourg on September 13.

> In fidelity to this teaching, in simple performance of the duty it
> imposes, guided and directed as well by other great figures over a
> wider range in our present and our past, the Governor General of
> Canada in silence and in dignity has done his part. His part being
> done, it has been my humble but proud privilege to stand at his side.

His eulogy of Charles Murphy, delivered in the Senate in 1936,
moved many a heart that day.

> But he whom he most revered in the past records of Canada was
> D'Arcy McGee. No one contributed so much to the immortality of
> that great figure in Canadian history as did Charles Murphy. He was a
> student of McGee for the same reason that he was a student of many
> other noted men. He himself had the same love of learning, the same
> poetic temperament, the same ardent patriotism.

Of McGee himself, at the famous one-hundredth-anniversary
dinner at the Château Laurier in Ottawa, Meighen said:

> But if Macdonald and Cartier were the architects of Confederation
> D'Arcy McGee was its prophet. He it was who in its grandest form
> caught the vision splendid; he it was who spread everywhere the
> fervour with which he was himself consumed; he it was whose rest-
> less pen and matchless platform power carried right into the hearts of
> the masses his message of tolerance and good will.

He concluded with these wise and prophetic words:

> And when distrust moves among us to estrange race from race, or
> class from class or to whisper in our ear that we are not our brother's
> keeper, let us listen over the hills to the reverberating eloquence, the
> lofty patriotism, the warm-hearted toleration, the wholesome wis-
> dom of Thomas D'Arcy McGee.

Thus Arthur Meighen, orator unrivalled at the summit of his powers, the qualities of mind and heart he attributed to McGee fitting no one better than himself.

THE RISE AND FALL OF R.B. BENNETT

To become Prime Minister of Canada it is not essential to have the assistance of a rich widow, although it helps. Jennie Shirreff, ten years older than R. B. Bennett, a police officer's daughter from the banks of the Miramichi, had known Bennett from childhood. She became the second wife and subsequently the widow of the fabulously rich Ezra Butler Eddy, founder of the Eddy Match Company and the Eddy Paper Company. On her death in 1921, Bennett got one-third of the estate. When her brother died a few years later, Bennett got the rest. With his other interests and investments, the Eddy estate guaranteed freedom from financial anxiety for the rest of his days.

I first got to know R.B. in 1911, when he appeared in the House as one of the new young Conservatives from the West; really he was an easterner from New Brunswick, one of the hard-nosed tribe of James Dunn, Isaak Walton Killam, and Beaverbrook, who took the world by the tail and never let go. Beaverbrook went on to the heights as a publisher and statesman in Britain and never forgot his boyhood friend. The story of their relationship and of Beaverbrook's boyish near-hero-worship of his older associate is told in that curious book, *Friends*, written by Lord Beaverbrook in 1958 after Bennett's death.

I was sitting there the night Arthur Meighen made a fool of R. B. Bennett in the 1914 debate on the resolution to grant the Canadian Northern Railway $40 million of new financing. It was like watching a ball bounce back and forth on a tennis court, Meighen expounding, Bennett breaking in with furious interruptions, which were handled coolly and disdainfully by the man from Portage la Prairie.

Bennett was a man of moods who seldom caught the ear of the House. As an orator he was powerful rather than persuasive. Meighen could run rings around him. In politics Bennett was a combination of Billy Graham and Jack the Ripper.

Bennett was impressed by pomp and ceremony. Like King he had a curious reverence for the opposite sex: his mother and his sister Mildred, a rather jolly, dashing woman, held a high place in his affections. He liked older women. He had a burning desire to hold centre stage and was always deeply moved at recognition accorded some poor but deserving person, no doubt a symbol of his own early frustrations. On one occasion, the consecration of Cardinal Villeneuve at the Basilica in Quebec City, Bennett's eyes filled with tears when the Cardinal's father was led down the main aisle to a front pew. He was not a consensus man; he was not above asking the opinions of others, he was only above accepting them.

He was nominated at the 1927 convention and was awarded the leadership when it became apparent Meighen was not in the running. Perhaps it is wise at this point to lay to rest the canard about Conservatives cannibalizing their own leaders. Meighen was absolutely determined to go. He had plans and ambitions for his family which could not be realized within the limits of party politics. He had devoted long years to his party and his country and felt that the time remaining belonged to his family. When Bennett appointed him to the Senate a few years later, he readily accepted. Manion and Bracken left after being ignominiously defeated; Drew was forced out by illness. John Diefenbaker was another story. The party felt it could not win under his leadership. Politics can be just that simple.

King had roundly defeated Meighen in 1926; but the manner of the defeat, the battle with Byng, the Bureau scandal, had taken almost as much out of King as it had out of the Conservatives. Four years later, in the face of economic crisis, the King government appeared a prisoner of lethargy and inactivity. King handed Bennett the 1930 election on a platter when he said he would not give a "five-cent piece" in depression relief to any province with a Conservative government. Bennett came back with 137 seats, 24 of them in Quebec. The Liberals under King had 88. The United

Farmers were down to 10 seats and the hodge-podge of Progressives, Liberal Progressives, Labour, and Independent Labour garnered 10 seats among them.*

Bennett was Prime Minister, a justification of everything he ever stood for. He was dogmatic with his Cabinet, and the story went around that when Bennett was seen walking down from Parliament Hill with his lips moving he was holding a one-man Cabinet meeting. In spite of his dislike for Bennett, King's respect for the office of prime minister was such that when Bennett became leader of the government King came into the House with him, holding Bennett by the arm and accompanying him to his seat. Some felt the display was a sign of King's reluctance to let go of the job.

King didn't have the same fear of Bennett that he had of Meighen. He could handle Bennett's bombast, but when Meighen's whip-lash comments crackled out over the Chamber, King crouched down in his seat.

Bennett had the reputation of being a dangerous man with the ladies. One day while he was still Leader of the Opposition, when the House was discussing a Doukhobor protest march in the Kootenays, a member launched at King the rhetorical question, what would the Prime Minister do if he came out on the porch at Kingsmere to find a group of naked women?

King replied quick as a flash, "I'd send for the Leader of the Opposition."

Bennett shot back the sharp reply that the Prime Minister was not known for sharing patronage with the other parties.

Bennett's lapses into heavy-footed humour were rather rare; he was noted for portentous solemnity. Before speaking he would glare round the Chamber from under straggly brows, pulling down sharply on the points of his waistcoat; then he would launch himself on a wave of bombastic prose, which members endured as best they might.

In 1932, in a bid to establish his international stature, Bennett

---

* In 1926 King had won 116 seats to Meighen's 91.

was host to the Imperial Economic Conference in Ottawa. The sessions droned on through hot July days, with R. J. Manion—a personable, likable M.P. who was to be Bennett's successor in the leadership—acting as spokesman with the press. Manion knew less than nothing about what was going on in the conference, and what little he knew he was not telling.

The British, in high hopes of securing what amounted to a common market with the Dominions, had sent a high-powered delegation led by two future prime ministers, Stanley Baldwin and Neville Chamberlain. Lord Runciman, President of the Board of Trade and an acknowledged expert on foreign trade, also attended. Beaverbrook wanted to send a special observer from London but Bennett, who happened to be on the outs with Beaverbrook at that moment, refused to have anything to do with Beaverbrook's man. Each day as the conference progressed, Bennett became more intransigent, more bombastic, and harder to get along with. Furiously, he attempted to impose his will on the men who ran the Empire.

The situation was not helped by the fact that, while Canadian journalists were limited to sweet nothings from Manion, the British journalists were getting complete reports from Runciman and Chamberlain at the Château Laurier each evening. Bennett was enraged when it was reported that Runciman and Chamberlain also found time to visit with Mackenzie King at his Kingsmere estate, where presumably they filled him in on the proceedings. The conference creaked to a miserable end with Bennett at one time requesting the C.P.R. to stand by with a vessel to convey the Britishers homeward if the atmosphere continued to deteriorate. Fortunately for the tattered shreds of Empire relationships this did not prove necessary.

On the rock of Bennett's intransigence the conference broke up in near disorder. Baldwin went back to England and blamed the Prime Minister of Canada. Neville Chamberlain conceived a detestation for Bennett so strong that when Beaverbrook attempted to secure a peerage for Bennett after his retirement, Chamberlain succeeded in blocking it. It was only after Winston Churchill became Prime Minister in 1941 that the "Beaver" was able to wangle Bennett's peerage through the Cabinet.

Incidentally, I was in Beaverbrook's home in those grim and resolute days and I recall Winston Churchill being on the telephone one evening at great length, obviously in the throes of some impassioned argument, and the "Beaver" giving back just as good as he got to the man who was to become the chief hope of freedom.

To revert to 1932, Bennett had certainly not endeared himself to the British. They left Ottawa feeling as though they'd been through some kind of mincing machine. Baldwin later quoted a former Liberal Cabinet minister: "Bennett has the manners of a Chicago policeman and the temperament of a Hollywood film star."

The shadow of depression crept across the land, lightened but dimly by the personality and confidence of Roosevelt: the mellifluous voice using the new medium of radio to encourage and bolster a panicky nation. The depression helped Bennett win the election; then it destroyed him. He had to find some means of coping with the collapse of confidence, of doing what Roosevelt and his imaginative and hard-hitting team of Harry Hopkins, Harold Ickes, General Hugh S. Johnson, Henry Wallace, and others were doing to lift the United States back up by its bootstraps.

The depression spread bitterness and fear, a penury western society had not seen since the seventeenth century, a turning back to social unrest. "Hallellujah, I'm a Bum", the firing on the bonus marchers in Washington by troops led by Douglas MacArthur, soup kitchens, riding the rods, farm foreclosures, good and decent men unable to feed their families—dismay and panic undreamed of in our day of affluence stalked across the land.

Roosevelt moved with vigour to stem the crisis, fighting loss of confidence with confidence ("The only thing we have to fear is fear itself"). Well, the fear was based on something real. To many it seemed as though a way of life was collapsing. Some profiteers got out with their investments; honest businessmen leaped from windows. Ordinary people were panic-stricken. Farmers as usual bore the brunt, and the long trek started from the land to the soup kitchens in the cities.

Roosevelt's "Bank Holiday" gave a breathing space to the hard-pressed economy; a series of far-reaching measures followed: w.p.a., which put all kinds of people to work at a living wage; the n.r.a. (National Recovery Act) under General Hugh Johnson, which marshalled business in the service of the Recovery; the c.c.c. (Civilian Conservation Corps), which sent young men into the woods to work on conservation. Dozens of presidential directives flowed out to cope with the challenge. Americans began breathing easier; the world's most resilient society was proving that it could adjust to disaster no less effectively than it adjusted to prosperity.

In Canada Bennett, with his advisers Bill Herridge and Rod Finlayson, and H. H. Stevens, his Minister of Trade and Commerce, sought for new and creative approaches. Herridge, married to Bennett's sister Mildred, was Canadian Minister to Washington, in an ideal situation to observe and note for Bennett's benefit the fine points of Roosevelt's recovery program.

He became friendly with Henry Agard Wallace, Roosevelt's Secretary of Agriculture, regarded even then as a bit of a radical. Wallace invited Bill Herridge to go to China with him, and Herridge, all enthusiasm, consented. Bennett heard about it, from Mildred no doubt, and put his foot down with a thump. No official of his government was travelling to China, and particularly not with anyone as radically inclined as Henry Wallace. Herridge continued to advise Bennett on how to cope with the depression.

He was assisted by Rod Finlayson, largely in his capacity as a speech writer. Rod practised law in Winnipeg and was a friend of John W. Dafoe, the Ottawa Valley boy who became the great editor of the *Winnipeg Free Press*. Dafoe was impressed with Finlayson's writing ability and his capacity for reducing political complexities to simple elements. Bennett, too, was impressed and brought Rod back east with him. Rod had ability but was short on political judgment; that is, his analysis of a given political situation was generally acute — it was in the solution that his perceptions began to wobble.

Rod was a master of the ringing phrase and Bennett, long accustomed to accepting briefs from juniors, did not always discriminate between what looked good on paper and what might prove effective in actual practice. He had before him the example of Roosevelt, who seemed able to mesmerize a nation with a phrase and wave away the goblins of despair with a magic wand of words. Bennett wanted to do the same.

Thus the genesis of such historical rodomontades as "We shall blast a way into the markets of the world" which goes down with King's "I wouldn't give them a five-cent piece", Diefenbaker's "No one will suffer from unemployment while I'm Prime Minister", Trudeau's "We'll wrestle inflation to the ground". They are the sort of outpourings which make dispassionate observers wonder whether Canadian politicians do not from time to time suffer from a tendency to become drunk on their speech-writers' prose.

Bennett hated liquor in any form, a prejudice not shared by Rod Finlayson, and he became furious one night when he walked into the Château Laurier cafeteria and found Rod standing on a table making a speech. But like a great many successful politicians Bennett discovered that you control people through their weaknesses, not their strength, and he developed a tolerance for weaknesses in those around him. With Rod and with Bill Herridge he could be himself, let his hair down, drop the mask of Empire-builder and statesman which he wore in public; he appreciated Rod's ability to dress up his rather mundane thoughts in sparkling prose. Rod stayed on after R.B. left, serving with Manion, Bracken, and George Drew, performing a service for the party that never received the appreciation it deserved.

Bennett inaugurated an ambitious plan of using federal public works to relieve unemployment. Nevertheless, the bold, sure measures to cope with poverty and despair were not forthcoming, and Bennett began to feel the pressure of failure. Meanwhile, King was waiting and planning and demanding action which Bennett was not in a position to provide.

You never knew where you stood with Bennett. Under the pressures of office and the daily-increasing demands of a society in economic disarray, Bennett's mercurial temperament became more uncertain than ever. When the *Ottawa Journal* ran an editorial criticizing the government, Bennett failed to recognize me. The next day he flung his arms around me.

Following the Imperial Economic Conference in Ottawa came the Disarmament Conference in Washington. Edouard Herriot represented France and Ramsay MacDonald was there as Prime Minister of Britain. Bennett, of course, represented Canada, ably seconded and advised by William Herridge. Among the clutch of Canadian reporters in Washington for the occasion, I was representing the *Ottawa Journal* and Grant Dexter the *Winnipeg Free Press*.

Bennett decided to hold a press conference in the Canadian Legation on Massachusetts Avenue. Dexter and I were late arriving. In one of the large reception rooms R.B. was surrounded by a crowd of American and Canadian reporters. I stopped for a word with Herridge, our Minister in Washington, and Grant went on to the group around R.B.

As soon as R.B. spotted Dexter he drew himself up as though confronted by a striking adder. "Ladies and gentlemen," he pontificated, "there will be no press conference. I refuse to say anything in the presence of Mr. Dexter, the emissary of John W. Dafoe of the *Winnipeg Free Press*, whose only purpose here is to distort and misrepresent Canada's position."

R.B. was having one of his feuds with Dafoe and decided to take it out on Dexter. Of course if Dafoe could have been present to hear R.B.'s ringing denunciation, he would have been delighted. For a few moments there was a stunned silence and the press rose and filed out. Herridge, a really nice person, stood there flabbergasted, trying to reason with R.B., a manifest impossibility once R.B.'s mind was made up.

I had never before heard a prime minister called a damn fool but on this occasion Herridge used strong words once the Americans were out of the room. He told R.B. that Dexter was one of the most honest journalists in Canada and that R.B. was just hurting himself. R.B. just stared stonily at the wall until we left.

Mildred Herridge did everything she could to repair the breach. She was a great girl, Bennett's sister, and R.B. thought the world of her, even though she was not above taking a drink from time to time. They had frequent fallings out, which usually ended with R.B. apologizing because he just couldn't get along without

Mildred's support and approval. Mildred, who often acted as R.B.'s hostess, was holding a reception at the Legation that night, and the Dexters were invited. Grant, of course, phoned and cancelled his acceptance. Mildred found out right away and called the hotel and talked to Grant's wife, Alice, who desperately wanted to go. Alice made some transparent excuse about having nothing to wear, so Mildred sent over a gown of her own by messenger from the Legation, brand new and never even worn. They were about the same size and so Alice Dexter no longer had any excuse for not going. They went and had a good time, with R.B. playing the perfect host as though nothing had happened. Grant Dexter was not mollified, however, and remained a dyed-in-the-wool Grit until the Pipeline Debate more than twenty years later changed an almost lifelong allegiance.

Bill Herridge didn't believe in paying too much attention to the State Department and the niceties of diplomatic backing and filling. He had Cabinet and Congressional contacts which provided a pipeline right into the White House. On occasion he gave interesting and informative breakfasts attended by people like Senators Borah and Hiram Johnson.

Bennett marched on indomitably toward the inevitable reckoning being prepared by King. At this point his march to destruction was hastened by a falling out with Harry Stevens, the one man in the party to whom Herridge's anti-business stand made an appeal. Stevens had failed in business and blamed the big boys for squeezing him out. He was quite prepared to blame the woes of the depression on conscienceless business practices and, in his job as Minister of Trade and Commerce, to tell business and industry to toe the line, which is what he proceeded to do.

Stevens chaired a parliamentary inquiry into price spreads and turned up scandalous profiteering by food distributors. He made a speech to a gathering of Conservative M.P.'s denouncing the way in which business was exploiting the public. It was a searing indictment, no worse perhaps in general theory than some of the references in Bennett's radio speeches, but with this difference: Stevens had minute documentation for every charge he made. Within a matter of weeks his speech found its way into a pamphlet. Meanwhile there was a steady "leakage" of information from the Price Spreads Inquiry, the Secretary of which, a young civil servant called Lester B. Pearson, brought himself to Bennett's attention by identifying the source of the leaks.

So much pressure was put on Bennett by his friends in business and industry that he wrote a note to Stevens demanding that he retract the charges attributed to him in his pamphlet. Stevens refused and in October 1934 resigned to head a new party, the Reconstruction Party.

In January, in an apparent attempt to head Stevens off at the pass, Bennett delivered a radio address which constituted a scathing attack on business in Stevens's language and in the very accent of Harry Stevens. It startled and frightened his friends and amused his enemies. Bennett introduced a series of acts to implement the recommendations of Stevens's Price Spread Inquiry, including a Wages and Hours Act, price and wage control, and extensive farm credit arrangements.

With Herridge and Finlayson preparing the speeches, Bennett embarked on a series of radio talks inaugurating a program of social reconstruction to meet the shattering problems of the depression. Some of the speeches were so radical that even R.B. was struck by the incongruity. Coming out of Cabinet one day he slapped the venerable Sir George Perley on the back. "How are you, comrade?" he quipped. Sir George was not amused.

The trouble with Bennett's speeches calling for a new social order was that Bennett didn't believe them himself, and it showed. Herridge and Finlayson would disappear to Herridge's cottage at Harrington Lake. After three or four days they would come back with another speech and R.B. would take to the airwaves, denouncing all the things he once believed in — unrestricted incomes, exploitation of resources, and so on. Roosevelt was gaining kudos with his attacks on "economic royalists" and R.B. wanted some of the same heady wine of success. Roosevelt was regarded as a traitor to his class for some of the things he said and did; he could live with the accusations and the bitterness, but R.B. was in a different position. For one thing, the people who felt that they were being attacked by R.B. were big contributors to the party. They honestly thought R.B. had taken leave of his senses. They felt put upon because they knew that capital in Canada was under far greater constraints than in the United States. Just the problem of attracting sources of capital created a very different atmosphere from the free-wheeling economy of the United States. On the other hand, the people R.B. hoped to reach, the little people affected by the depression, the middle class with their savings wiped out, were not impressed because they just didn't believe a damn word R.B. was saying.

Bennett had a dreadful fear of being tarred with Herbert Hoover's brush and being brought down in failure for lack of a program of popular appeal. He launched the Canadian Radio Broadcasting Commission (forerunner of the Canadian Broadcasting Corporation) in an attempt to "Canadianize" the airwaves. Meanwhile Herridge supplied the philosophy, the ideological thrust, mostly directed against business and industry, and Rod Finlayson provided words and phrases.

The differences between Bennett and Stevens were more than merely political. Bennett was a bit of a snob. He appeared everywhere in top hat and striped trousers and morning coat. Stevens had no time for that sort of nonsense. Bennett was a High Tory posturing as a Roosevelt Democrat. Stevens was a type to be met with on the Labour benches in England. He was quite a bit closer to Bill Herridge's type of thinking than he was to Bennett's. But then, Herridge could say things nobody else could; Stevens didn't happen to be married to Bennett's sister.

In the federal election of 1935 Bennett went down to defeat. While he succeeded to an extent in drawing Stevens's fangs he was nevertheless unable to convince the voters of the effectiveness of his own proposals. Stevens was the only member of the Reconstruction Party to get a seat. The reason was, of course, that his candidates were unknown mediocrities. Had they all been of Stevens's calibre, he would have made a different showing. He had hoped to pick up the adherents of the fragmented Progressive movement. However, the farm vote, perhaps logically, did not turn to a big-city type like Harry Stevens. Instead it went to two new parties: Social Credit, inaugurated in Alberta under the messianic leadership of William "Bible Bill" Aberhart; and the c.c.f.

under J. S. Woodsworth, depression-bred, an outgrowth of the Winnipeg Strike and the Regina Manifesto. The Liberals under a revivified Mackenzie King shot up to 171 seats, while the Conservatives sagged to a rock-bottom low of 39, of which 25 were in. Ontario.* Dark times loomed for the Conservative Party at Ottawa.

King learned more from the depression than Bennett did. One of the things King learned was that even in a time of social crisis change must be measured in accordance with the country's capacity to adjust to it. In each speech Bennett threw out a bewildering succession of nostrums, most of them impractical or borrowed from Roosevelt. King, on the other hand, proceeded cautiously, inching his way into social reconstruction. He borrowed much of his social program from the Progressives and the c.c.f. and calmly took the credit for reforms which he instituted as a measure of self-preservation.

The second reason for Bennett's defeat was his own personality. C. H. Cahan, one of his ministers, made the statement that "the sun never sets on the day on which the Prime Minister hasn't insulted some good and loyal Conservative."

After Bennett's defeat the Conservative Party lost little time in throwing him from the battlements. This was one case in which a leader, who with a little encouragement might have stayed on, was sent packing, to go into exile in England with his melancholy memories and a peerage.

Here again, R.B. was in a sense hoist with his own petard. He was always threatening to resign. "I'll go!" he'd say and wait for the objections to pour in. After the defeat in 1935 there were no objections. While Herridge exhorted the delegates at Lansdowne Park not to turn their backs on Bennett, R.B. sat by the telephone in his suite in the Château Laurier. The phone didn't ring. The party went about its business of electing R. J. Manion.

There comes a time in the progression of political succession when it is manifested by a kind of universal instinct that a leader can make no more constructive contribution than to remove him-

* (1935) Liberal 171, Conservative 39, Social Credit 17, c.c.f. 7, Others 11. In 1930 the Conservatives had taken 137 seats, the Liberals 88.

self from the leadership. Some leaders are slow to appreciate this sometimes unpalatable but wholesome truth. Meighen did not need to be told when it was time to go. Mr. King, on the other hand, having ensured the succession through the election of Louis St. Laurent as party leader, continued to cling to the prime-ministership and even went to London to attend a Prime Ministers' Conference. Mr. St. Laurent, unbeatable in 1953, was a liability in 1957, his "Uncle Louis" image tattered and disordered with age, and it was left to Mike Pearson to be the one to tell him so.

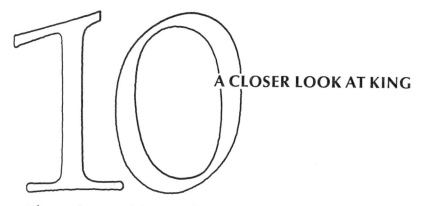

A CLOSER LOOK AT KING

The posthumous life of Mackenzie King is an extraordinary thing in our political story.

Canada celebrated his centennial in 1974. But when did we celebrate the centennial of Laurier, or of Borden, not to mention King's two antagonists, Bennett and Meighen? I, around Parliament close to forever, cannot recall anything like this. There is a Parliament Hill monument to King, but none to Bennett or Meighen.

More books have been written about Mackenzie King than about any of the Fathers of Confederation. Historians, biographers, memoirists, commentators, and publicists fall over each other in writing about him, mostly in paeans of praise, often hyperbolically.

I have read every line of King's published diaries. I have to say, without prejudice, for I liked the old scoundrel, that they are not worth two pieces; they recalled for me Felix Frankfurter's remark that "as a source of history, diaries aren't worth a damn." Actually this is a record of housekeeping of the Liberal Party under King, with God an invisible pilot. A few years ago they had a series of books in England on *Curiosities in Politics*. If we ever have similar volumes in Canada, King's diaries would be a rich field.

I knew Mackenzie King long before he became leader of the Liberal Party and Prime Minister; I knew him when he was getting out the *Canadian Liberal* for his party; I sat through the 1919 Liberal convention which made him leader; and I watched and heard him from the Press Gallery as Opposition Leader and Prime Minister during the years of his reign, years when he gave Conservatives a new meaning of eternity.

He was not a great parliamentarian, not an orator, not even a great debater. He was without Churchill's armoury of words, lacked Laurier's "proud full sail", and was incapable of Meighen's searing invective and glittering impromptus.

Only once, as I remember, did he rise above himself—the year 1926, when, during the election campaign over the Byng incident, he became the grandson of the old rebel and spoke with a degree of passion and power. In vain did we plead with Meighen to answer him; Meighen, who underestimated him, and sincerely thought of him as an unfathomable fraud, ignored his charges — to his sorrow. King won that election on the platform.

Why did he keep on winning?

Acton's answer of collective mediocrity, applied to the long reign of Lord Liverpool, "he was successful not despite his mediocrity, but because of it", is too easy. Greatness is not easily defined. Nor craftiness. Great or not, some men become leaders, some do not, and among those who do there are qualitative differences. Mackenzie King had these differences.

King was often shrewd, seldom profound, sometimes superficial. His basic instinct was political survival. Around that all else revolved. That he suffered from deep inner insecurity and a classical fear of death shows up on every page of his diaries and in his embrace of spiritualism. He banished his fear of death by convincing himself that death did not exist, that he could converse with and get messages from his mother and even from his dog. Some wag has suggested that for a period the affairs of the country were run by the shade of King's terrier, Pat. Another wag topped this by suggesting the present government should make every effort to get in touch with Pat.

On the eve of the Liberal convention of 1948, which chose Louis St. Laurent to replace Mackenzie King, I indulged in some reminiscing on the *Ottawa Journal's* editorial page.

> We've been wondering how many of the Liberal faithful who are in Ottawa today waiting for Mr. King to tell them what's in store for them in the way of leadership, remember back to the convention of 29 years ago which gave them Mr. King? . . . ·

It was the day of Charley Murphy and Andrew Haydon and Jacques Bureau and Ernest Lapointe, men who all but believed in the second coming of Laurier. . . .

There is a legend now—no doubt many of the young Liberals who are in Ottawa today have come to believe it—that in 1919 Mr. Mackenzie King was the overwhelming choice for the party's leadership. Actually and more especially outside Quebec, he wasn't. Ontario wanted Fielding, as did convention leaders like Nova Scotia's George Murray and most of the men from the Maritimes and the West.

Fielding had been Laurier's chief captain, had stood beside him as his Finance Minister through 15 years; they would forget his support of conscription. Mr. King, on the other hand, was comparatively unknown. He had been a reporter on the Toronto Globe, had gone from Toronto University to the University of Chicago (where legend said he had once won, of all things, a foot race), had studied at Jane Addams' Hull House and at Harvard and had been a protege of Mulock's and our first Minister of Labour . . .

Yet Mr. King in the end got the prize, though those who were there knew that he got it only because Quebec wanted him and he was able to add to that support the best speech of the convention. . . .

Of the years that followed much secret history remains to be written. The reasons behind the selection of Meighen to succeed Borden; the debacle of the Conservatives (who had already begun changing their label) in 1921; the rise and fall of the Progressives under T. A. Crerar; the secret negotiations that went on between A. B. Hudson and Crerar and Andrew Haydon and others to have the Progressives join with the Liberals; the Beauharnois "valley of humiliation" episode of which Wilfrid Laurier McDougald and Haydon were made the scapegoats; the Customs scandal which the Conservatives muffed by being too much in a hurry to take office; the "constitutional" election which shadowed the last days in Canada of Lord Byng; the behind-the-scenes intrigues against King which, when better days returned (better than the Liberal low ebb of 1925-26), left many a Liberal captain in the doghouse—all these things remain to be told. . . .

Well, they still have not been told in full, nor are they likely to be, because the people who could fill in the details are either dead or discreetly silent.

Meighen, with his crystal-clear mind, saw King as a poseur and a charlatan playing the role of a brooding intellectual, an unscrupulous nonentity who seized the mantle from Laurier—and him not yet cold—to wrap it vaingloriously about himself.

King hated Meighen because Meighen failed to take him seriously. Meighen saw him for what he was, a pompous little man with an urge for power. He was, of course, more than that; and Meighen found that out. Meighen's contempt, never hidden, was not political but personal, a manifestation of disdain. Once King got power, he put intellectual pretensions aside and contented himself with dealing with day-to-day problems by pitting one segment of the country against another, a tribal approach worthy of the leader of a developing African nation.

King's modest appraisal of his own efforts set out in his diary was, "I have led the Party with vigour, with insight and judgment." Whether he had done as much for the country remained open to question.

Mackenzie King's deep inner insecurity, which led him to spiritualism, also gave insights into what the Canadian people would accept. There was no way in which he was prepared to risk Quebec support, Laurier's legacy, the sure and essential guarantee of his political survival. He clung to Quebec for political and sentimental reasons and reduced the political impact of the province to a nation of pallbearers perpetuating the demise of Wilfrid Laurier.

Victory came to King standing on the twin planks of Laurier's legacy and the horrid Conservative iniquity of conscription. Momentarily dislodged by Meighen, upset by Bennett and economic collapse, he never again after 1935 looked on the dreary face of defeat.

Like a latter-day Merlin, he achieved his effects by black magic, gobbling up opponents such as Manion and Bracken like a Minotaur devouring young virgins. Through the years, as the Liberal Party accumulated victories it accumulated power, created vested interests — a party establishment that stretched through the tight-knit cordons of government. The bright young men with career intentions who knew which side their careers were buttered on went where the power was; and the mavericks and those who believed in a two-party system, however creaking, went the other way.

King could neither read, write, nor speak a word of French, yet held Quebec in the hollow of his hand for years. How? To Norman Lambert, president of the Liberal Federation, he would say: "Lambert, keep your hands off Quebec; leave Quebec to Lapointe, Cardin, and Chubby Power." King was shrewd enough to let Lapointe run the party machinery in Quebec, building an unbeatable machine on the bones of Louis Riel and the mothers' sons sent across the seas against their will to fight a foreign foe. The Quebec syndrome which guaranteed twenty-two years of uninterrupted power for the Liberals under King and St. Laurent had a brief interruption when Maurice Duplessis used his personal power to turn the province over to Diefenbaker, but worked again for Pearson after Duplessis was gone, as it is working now for Trudeau.

The need for Quebec support explained King's dithering on conscription, his incredible and paradoxical contradictions, his waffling in the Customs scandal in which a Quebec minister was involved, his launching out into the deeps of a constitutional crisis with Byng, knowing Quebec would vote on the issue with a single mind while the rest of the country was divided. The secret of Liberal success since Laurier can be summed up with a slight modification of Teddy Roosevelt's dictum: "Walk softly and carry a big Quebec stick."

King was withdrawn, devious, subtle, his character never fully known or appreciated by the Canadian people; in the war years a figure seen at international conferences, at Hyde Park with Roosevelt, engrossed in great affairs; then, the great issues laid aside, scuttling away to confer in secret with one of the many mediums, invariably female, to whom he turned for reassurance.

King came on the Ottawa scene in 1900 as editor of the *Labour Gazette* and soon became Deputy-Minister of Labour. In 1918 he published *Industry and Humanity*, a turgid exposition of his views on labour relations and collective bargaining. He is given credit for being the architect of the Industrial Disputes Investigations

Act, for years the charter of organized labour in Canada, pickled in amber by the Labour Department, whose Liberal loyalists would not hear of altering a single syllable. For years after King left the office in the Confederation Building where he held forth as Canada's first Labour Minister, everything was preserved exactly as he left it.

King had a friend, perhaps the only really intimate friend of his entire life spent among politicians and relics of the dead. Henry Albert Harper was an employee of the Labour Department who drowned in the Ottawa River while trying to save a young girl. In commemoration of this tragic event, King had erected a rather bulbous granite monument showing a young and dashing Sir Galahad; this now stands on Wellington Street in the City of Ottawa, largely ignored by passers-by, who are unaware of its whimsical and curious origin. The monument may represent (apart from his devotion to his dog) the one and only outburst of pure sentimentality on King's part.

King was a combination of sensitivity and toughness. He panted for power as pants the hart for cooling streams. It was necessary to compensate for some deficiency in his make-up. I remember a learned study which sought an explanation for the contradictions in Mackenzie King in a personality conflict arising out of the fact that his maternal grandfather, William Lyon Mackenzie, was on one side in the 1837 rebellion while his paternal ancestor fought for the government. According to this theory, very large numbers of people in the United States, whose ancestors fought on opposing sides in both the Revolutionary War and the Civil War, should by now be psychopathic cases because of the endless pattern of conflicts that was set up.

The real explanation of King's aberrations (which he successfully kept out of his political judgments) — the visits to mediums, his communication with his mother and others, his fetish about making decisions when the hands of the clock were at either twenty to or twenty after the hour, his exaggerated attachment to his dog in life and death — appears to stem in some curious way from his feelings about his mother, not an unusual preoccupation with great men, particularly politicians.

King's relationship with his mother, outlasting her life, surpassed the average regard of a son for his mother. If there is such a thing as an Oedipus complex, King's was a classic case; if there is no such thing, it would have to be invented to explain Mackenzie King. He had pictures of his mother hung on the walls of his office in the Centre Block. He consulted her regularly, as his diary shows. When he pulled off a particularly Machiavellian piece of business, he felt Mother was happy. The real explanation of his almost superstitious attachment to the memory of his grandfather, that grand old rebel William Lyon Mackenzie, apart from obvious political dividends, was that William Lyon Mackenzie enjoyed the holy privilege of being the father of Mackenzie King's mother.

It was only after King's death and, indeed, after publication of hitherto excised sections of his diary that the stories came out full flower about his dabbling in spiritualism. Although many people knew and even hinted about his curious aberrations, most of it was shoved under the rug during his lifetime. You don't quarrel with success. As far as his fellow Liberals were concerned—those who had the best opportunity to know what was going on—it wouldn't do at all to let it get about that the Prime Minister of the country, the leader of the party for nearly thirty years, was a frequenter of mediums and a gazer into crystal balls when he wasn't busy communicating with the shades of departed friends. In any case, as long as King kept on winning elections the leading Liberals were not about to complain. Such was King's hold on the party that they were more likely to take up the same practices themselves.

The spiritualistic aspect of King, carefully concealed from all but a few intimates during his lifetime, became a matter of public notoriety when the complete diaries were opened to inspection, in contrast to earlier versions published under the authority of J. W. Pickersgill, who apparently allowed himself to be guided by the hand of the master in the manner of the chroniclers of Holy Writ. In the unexpurgated diaries, replete with spiritualistic references, even the Deity emerges as the unseen organizer of Liberal victories. King's ego shines forth in an entry following Winston

Churchill's famous "Iron Curtain" speech at Fulton, Missouri. "Being my grandfather's grandson, I should today be speaking to the countries of the world as Churchill is speaking."

Thus the naked ego speaks. Regardless of whose grandson he might be, Mackenzie King never saw the day when he was in the same street as an orator with Winston Churchill. His attachment to clichés and convoluted verbosity were such that in his entire public career, the longest in the British Empire, one looks nearly in vain for a single clear, definite statement.

Something of the real Mackenzie King came out recently when the public was regaled with such curiously macabre scenes as, for example, the burial party, complete with hymn singing, of his dog, at Kingsmere.

One of the most amusing entries in the unexpurgated diaries relates the appearance of Borden and Meighen in a vision, apologizing to King for the statement that he offered himself for Sir Robert Borden's Union Government in 1917 and was turned down. This story infuriated King all through his political life, and he went to great lengths to lay it by the heels, probably on account of its absolute truth. I had the story from Meighen himself and there is no doubt whatever that King offered his services to Borden in 1917. King, of course, had this wonderful advantage that whatever went wrong in the world around him he was able to put right in the spirit world, sanctioned by his mother's mystic applause and the silent approval of the spheres.

When the Germans were at the gates of Paris in the First World War, the French were frantically trying to negotiate a war loan in Washington. From an unimpeachable source I got the story that King, then a labour advisor for the Rockefellers at twenty thousand a year, wrote a letter to William Jennings Bryan, the Secretary of State, to advise that France should not be granted the loan. An inveterate meddler even then.

Clothing himself in the trappings of reform and the New Socialism, King in actual fact instituted old age pensions in 1927 only under pressure from J. S. Woodsworth. He ruthlessly stole planks from the Progressives and later from the C.C.F., and even from the Conservatives. Out of the ordinary run of men, set apart in spite of himself by baffling characteristics, the counterpoint of his personality was the driving need for personal security.

I see King, tears dimming his eyes, crying in the House over his poverty, his inability to entertain members. Once he gave a maid at Laurier House a dressing down for giving a cup of tea to the policeman on the beat. He wasn't buying tea for policemen. After his death his will was probated at a million dollars. He had an unconcealed dislike for any Conservative leader who showed even a spark of ability. In Meighen and Bennett he saw the possibilities of his own defeat. In Manion's case he could afford to show a kind of patronizing contempt.

Writing in the *Ottawa Journal* in August 1970, I described Mackenzie King as he seemed to me:

> ... an extraordinary combination of sentimentality and toughness, of tenderness and cruelty, of monastic exclusiveness and political sophistication. Not before or since have we had a politician like him.

Yet King could show understanding and sympathy. When our son was reported missing in the war King sent a deeply considerate telegram to me and my wife; when his death on active duty was confirmed we received a long, compassionate letter from the Prime Minister, revealing a side of the man entirely other than most people suspected. On another occasion, when I was Ottawa Editor of the old *Collier's* magazine, a visiting editor came to Ottawa and the Prime Minister went out of his way to entertain him; he had him to lunch at Laurier House and in general treated him like royalty. There was nothing in it for Mackenzie King; it was just a way of doing me a purely gratuitous good turn. These things are not forgotten.

As far as his ministers were concerned, like many single-minded wielders of power, he was capable of tolerating the frailties of those around him, compensating in his own mind, no doubt, by his own strength for their weaknesses. He preferred to have around him people who owed their position to him rather than to their own brilliance. Some of his ministers drank and this was a handle to control them by; others had other problems. King was the only one with no problems and if he had any, no one would know about them.

He was not able to tolerate Ralston's placing his conscience in the conscription crisis above the collective responsibility of the Cabinet. He dismissed him out of hand, replacing him with McNaughton, who couldn't get elected. Then King sat by coolly and watched McNaughton being ripped to shreds in the House defending a military policy of which he was not the author, his whilom glory hanging in rags and tatters. But King was saved.

Years later, from Louis St. Laurent, I got the true story of King's duplicity in that crisis. His remarks were not made under the seal of the confessional and I summarize them here.

The general outlines of the conscription crisis are well known. Conscription, imposed in the First World War, hung like an albatross around the Conservative Party's neck for over thirty years. It was used to defeat me in Gaspé. The Liberal Party, conscious of its alliance with Quebec, swore over and over there would never again be conscription in Canada.

When war broke out in 1939, King brought in National Registration, a pallid enough measure; but even that caused a bit of an uproar in Quebec, as people like Camillien Houde, the Mayor of Montreal, went around telling people not to register. King was deathly afraid that events would pressure him into a situation in which the conscription issue would have to be faced, and with the awful obstinacy of insecure people made up his mind he would never allow himself to be saddled with the stigma of heading a Liberal government which introduced outright conscription.

As the war widened, casualties grew on land, at sea, and in the air. King compromised with a National Service Policy, which called up Canadians for home service or service within Canada's territorial waters.

The so-called "Zombie" army was not very successful. People called up for home service resented it about as much as if they had been conscripted for overseas; and at the same time the crying need for overseas reinforcements was not being met. King then had recourse to the solution proposed by Arthur Meighen seventeen years earlier and derided by King. He called a plebiscite in order that the Canadian people might liberate him from his undertaking not to impose conscription for overseas service. The results were instructive. Overwhelmingly, English Canada voted to give the government a free hand to bring in full conscription, and almost as overwhelmingly Quebec voted against. No action was taken, and the situation became acute in 1944 when J. L. Ralston, the Minister of Defence, went overseas and found that Canadian units were operating in the firing lines below strength and without proper reinforcements. At this point General McNaughton, the Canadian commander overseas, was brought back, partly as a result of falling out with the British and partly because King needed him to replace Ralston, whom he summarily fired.

That was the background to the crisis brought on when King decided finally that there was no way out. Conscription must be imposed. He would lose through resignation Quebec ministers like Cardin and Power. He had already lost Ralston, of course, by kicking him out. General McNaughton was a slender reed for King to lean on in any *political* sense; his political knowledge was on the level of the rawest subaltern in his army, and he could not get elected.

That left Louis St. Laurent, King's Minister of Justice, the outstanding French Canadian of his day. If St. Laurent walked out, the government was finished; if St. Laurent could be persuaded to stay and support conscription, all was not lost.

Late one night King called St. Laurent to his office and told him bluntly there was danger of a military takeover unless the troops could be reinforced through conscription. When St. Laurent told me the story sitting in his apartment in the Roxborough over three years later he still couldn't be sure whether King meant what he said.

"What could I do?" Expressive Gallic shrug. "I had to pretend I believed him. I even had to pretend that I believed that he himself believed what he was saying. Is that too complicated? In any event, it made no real difference. I had already made up my mind that conscription must come. There was no other way. It was just a question of when and how."

King had been categorical in his affirmation of the coming revolt of the military. "I have information from the most reliable source," he told St. Laurent. "The Army may rise up against the Government if steps are not taken to fill up the battalions overseas." St. Laurent looked at me with his tight little smile. "You know the top brass in the Army, O'Leary, and so do I. Do you think it is likely they were ready to revolt?'

I said I hadn't heard anything about it; nevertheless, everyone knew the situation in 1944 was pretty ticklish. King's reliable source must have been McNaughton, I suggested. St. Laurent nodded. "Obviously, some kind of ultimatum was conveyed to King. He seemed sincerely afraid that we were on the borderline of anarchy."

"He should have been afraid," I said. "After all, his refusal to deal with the issue created the situation in the first place."

King said he had authentic information the Chiefs of Staff were no longer in control. There was a definite possibility of civil war. All across Canada the military were demanding action. It was conscription or else. Sitting there in St. Laurent's apartment, having a drink with him, the story seemed to me a wild chimera out of the distant past.

"He was deadly serious," St. Laurent said. "I assured him of my full support because I had already decided on my course." Obviously King didn't want the kind of dilemma that smashed the Liberals under Laurier in 1917. It wasn't the state of public order King was worrying about but the state of the Liberal Party in Quebec.

"I gave him the impression that I believed the situation was as he described it," St. Laurent said. "I was really quite sceptical. King appeared satisfied with my reaction and within a few days we brought in conscription."

Peace in Europe came that spring. King had delayed conscription long enough so that when it came it had little practical effect in either a military or a political sense. He risked his Cabinet and managed to save his government. There were some who felt that a lot of Canadians died who needn't have, if King had had the courage to do what was necessary at the time when it was needed.

In the fall of 1941 the British government sponsored a trip by Canadian newspapermen to afford them a first-hand glimpse of the war effort. Arthur Ford of the *London Free Press*, Bishop Renison, who was writing for the Toronto *Globe*, Jean-Louis Gagnon of *La Presse*, Lionel Shapiro, who wrote the best-selling *Sixth of June*, and B. K. Sandwell of *Saturday Night* were among those invited.

In those wartime days the flight was a roundabout one, New York to Bermuda, then to the Azores. You were lucky if you weren't sent back to Bermuda (as we were when halfway to the Azores) by rumours of enemy activity. The crossing took three days. We were met in Lisbon by Michael Stewart, who later became Foreign Secretary in the Labour government. London was deep in the blackout. They put us up in the Savoy and the British looked after everything. We did a lot of travelling in England, mostly at night, no lights on. We went to Aldershot and other places where Canadian soldiers were stationed.

They said I must see Cardinal Hinsley. Next to Churchill he was the most listened-to man in England. So one day they sent a car for me and I went to visit Cardinal Hinsley, a tall, fine-looking man. I bent to kiss his ring and he said, "Nonsense, come here and sit down." I liked that.

He said, "You'll be going to Ireland?"

"Yes."

"Will you be seeing De Valera?"

I expected I would. Brendan Bracken had arranged everything. Hinsley hitched his scarlet gown forward. "I want you to ask Dev three questions: First, why did he suppress one of my sermons? Next, why has he stopped allowing wool to the women knitting socks for the Irish soldiers in the British army? And last, how does he explain that he sent fire brigades from Dublin to put out the fires in Belfast when the German bombs fell, in spite of a threat by the German Ambassador to bomb Dublin itself if that happened again?" The Cardinal was a well-informed man. I promised I would put the questions exactly as he phrased them.

When I was shown into De Valera's office he came from behind the desk with his hand out.

93

"I presume you're of Irish descent."

What a thing to say to me. I said, "Mr. De Valera, there isn't one drop of blood in my veins that isn't Irish."

"Well," he said, "you have the advantage over me."

I said, "I'm sorry I opened my mouth and put my foot in it."

He laughed with great good nature and said I'd given him a story to amuse his colleagues. He had an Irish face with the nose and the long upper lip, like an Irish academician, and tight-brushed, wiry hair. You could hardly imagine the man carrying a gun in the Easter Rebellion, imprisoned by the British, and all the rest. Until you saw his eyes. At the same time he was a consummate politician, the blood of Ireland ripe in his veins although he was born in the United States.

I gave him Cardinal Hinsley's three questions and he smiled a little grimly and answered with some care. "In answer to the first, tell the Cardinal what he full well knows. It wasn't a sermon I suppressed but a British Army recruiting speech. As for the second question, I have no objection to Irish women knitting for the soldiers, especially Irish soldiers. Are you sure it isn't for British uniforms he wants Irish wool?"

"And if they are on Irish backs?"

"You would have made a good bishop yourself," he said.

Wool was scarce and had to be controlled and that was all there was to it. I said, "What about the German Ambassador and him threatening to bomb Dublin?"

At that, I saw the fire in his eyes. "I was awakened in the small hours before dawn and told of the bombing of Belfast and the city on fire. When an Irish city's on fire, O'Leary, no matter in what part of Ireland, it's our duty to help put it out. If the German Ambassador complains to me, which he hasn't, about my sending up the fire brigades from Dublin, I'll kick him out of my office."

Some people objected to the editorials I wrote defending Irish neutrality in the last war. In the first place, it didn't hurt Britain's effort to have Ireland neutral. In the second, the British forces were swarming with Irish. In the third, wasn't it what the Commonwealth was about, freedom of choice? Wasn't it in fact what the war was about?

94

The same people who couldn't understand how I could defend Ireland couldn't understand how I could defend Quebec. There is such a thing as a minority viewpoint. This is something you learn as an Irish Catholic or a French Canadian. I happen to believe a minority viewpoint has a right to be expressed and treated with respect.

When I got back to London the British threw a luncheon for us at the Savoy. Cardinal Hinsley was there. "Did you see Dev?' he asked.

"Yes, I did."

"What did he say about suppressing my sermon?'

"Well, he said he didn't suppress a sermon, it was a recruiting speech."

"Ah," he said, and went off without waiting for the other two answers. His expression was curiously like De Valera's when I put the questions, grimly sardonic. Oh, the age-old and tenuous bridge between Irishmen on opposite sides of the same question.

Another distinguished guest at the same luncheon was Viscount Bennett, a little stouter and very much the exile, though he hadn't aged much. He inquired about the party's chances under Manion. He wanted to know all about Meighen, Mackenzie King, leading figures in politics and industry. He seemed weary and a little disillusioned. I had the impression he would have liked to return and pick up life in Canada, but only on his own terms. His sister Mildred had died in 1938 and this was a grievous loss. That was the last time I saw Bennett.

That night there was a bombing. It wasn't much of a bombing but every window in the hotel was broken. We had to sleep on the floor because there was glass everywhere, and always the chance they might come back. B. K. Sandwell and I were sharing a room and all we could hear was the sound of shovels scraping up broken glass. What I saw in Britain shattered the state of euphoria many of us had indulged in about conditions in England. Canadian and American journalists were coming back and writing about "business as usual", Britain "muddling through", and all that sort of bosh. They were doing the British people a disservice.

The truth was that the British people, noble and gallant as they were, were suffering. Food was being rationed, children were being sent out of London, bombing raids were taking place with alarming frequency, and not all of the ringing hyperbole of Churchill's "Give us the tools and we will finish the job" could alter the simple fact that Britain's back was against the wall.

I wrote of being in Westminster listening to Churchill speak:

> The speech for the most part was more for home than world consumption, was an answer to the critics who demand that Britain do more about Russia. As Mr. Churchill got to grips with these he became more vigorous, used his armoury of wit and sarcasm with devastating effect. This was the old House of Commons warrior using all the arts and tricks he has learned through the years and plainly enjoying himself thoroughly.

At Churchill's press conference afterwards, I was impressed by his gaiety in the midst of earth-shaking events, his "clear love of mischief and fun, his Puckish, humorous face". Who can forget his visit to Ottawa when, at the very height of the war, he told a packed Canadian House of Commons how Hitler had misjudged the tenacity and determination of the democracies, particularly Britain, whose neck he had promised to wring "like a chicken" — and the snarl in the famous bulldog voice when he growled out, "Some chicken! Some neck!"

All the talk about McNaughton's Canadian Army "like a dagger at the heart of Berlin" could not change the truth. After Dunkirk Britain stood helpless as a bird before the overwhelming and ruthless force of Nazi Germany.

I spoke to the Canadian Club in Ottawa at a luncheon attended by the biggest crowd the Canadian Club had had up to that time. I said Britain could not finish the job with tools alone: the Nazis would not be beaten until Canada and America sent their young men to do the job as in 1914 and 1917.

After the luncheon Mackenzie King, who was present, came up and congratulated me. "As Prime Minister, I could not say what you said; but I agree completely and I think your saying it will do some good."

DREW, ST. LAURENT, AND HOWE

Bennett was succeeded as party leader by R. J. Manion, a charming man whose personality was so lacking it was not even possible
to dislike him. The party wiseacres felt that because his wife was
French-Canadian this would help Manion break into Quebec. He
barely broke into Ontario. In the 1940 election the Conservatives
ended up with 39 seats after attempting the ploy that had worked
for Borden in 1917, National Government.* Manion, unfortunately, wasn't Borden or even Bennett. Manion, at best a light
skirmisher, was followed by John Bracken, an amiable disaster.

Bracken's political antecedents were, to say the least, curious.
Generally regarded as a Liberal, he succeeded in becoming
Premier of Manitoba as head of a coalition. I said to Meighen (who
had, the year before, come out of the Senate to resume the leadership but had then failed to win a seat in the House), "Why are you
foisting this disaster on the Party?" Meighen said, "We have lost
the Quebec vote and the labour vote. With Bracken we will at least
keep the farm vote." This was an exercise in over-optimism. Even
the farmers wouldn't vote for Bracken. The candidates at the 1942
Convention in Winnipeg included John Diefenbaker, Howard
Green, M. M. Macpherson, and Harry Stevens. Bracken rode
over them all, although up to the last minute he had the appearance of a man being taken for a ride.

Bracken insisted that the word Progressive should be tacked on
to the Conservative Party. I was very much against enlarging a

---

*(1940) Liberal 178, Conservative 39, Social Credit 10, C.C.F. 8, Others 10.
This is the same number of seats (39) the Conservatives had won in 1935.

party name which was good enough for Borden and Meighen and Bennett. I brought up the matter again in 1945 when I said, "There have been too many christenings." But the name stayed as amended by Bracken, his only legacy to the Progressive Conservative Party.

With Bracken in the 1945 election we pushed our seats up to 67, 48 in Ontario. The great fragmentation of the anti-Liberal opposition was under way. The c.c.f. got 28 seats, 18 of them in Saskatchewan, and the Social Credit came back with 13 in Alberta. Each of these seats was, in effect, a gain for the Liberal Party, simply because it meant one less for the Conservatives.*

The prize for the most ineffectual Conservative leader in my time would be a toss-up between Manion and Bracken. Bracken did reasonably well on farm questions, but once he strayed from the back forty he was lost. On one occasion, delivering a speech on the economy prepared for him by Rod Finlayson, he bitterly attacked the effects of a certain excise tax. The Minister of Finance, the urbane Douglas Abbott, rose in his seat and reminded Mr. Bracken that the government had announced removal of the tax that morning. Bracken went right on with the speech as written, attacking the tax which no longer existed, incapable of changing gears once he was in motion.

Bracken withdrew with a little more finesse than when he entered the leadership; he went out to Manotick near Ottawa and raised palomino horses with considerably greater success than he had shown in raising the voters.

His exit set the stage for George Drew, who did more than anyone since Bennett to restore the Conservative Party as a fighting opposition, organized and keyed up to defend individual rights and the enterprise system. I knew and admired George Drew as Premier of Ontario. He trusted me and asked my advice. As a speaker, he was in a class by himself, with a booming voice and excellent command of language. His weakness was that he had no terminal facilities.

---

*(1945) Liberal 125, Progressive Conservative 67, c.c.f. 28, Social Credit 13, Others 12.

Drew was personally impressive, with an unfortunate capacity for sometimes sounding on a platform like a stuffed shirt. He was anything but that. He came from a prominent family in Guelph; one of his progenitors and a namesake sat behind John A. Macdonald in Parliament and articled under John Sandfield Macdonald.

Drew attended Upper Canada College, a private school for boys on the English public-school model, and entered law. He was wounded in the First World War, leaving him with a stiff arm which most people were unaware of. He served briefly as an aide to Lord Bessborough, where his tall, handsome physique and engaging personality made him an adornment to the Governor General's staff. He wrote a reasonably successful book popularizing Canada's part in the First World War. If he had not dedicated himself to politics, he would have made an outstanding journalist. For a brief period he was Chairman of the Ontario Securities Commission.

In 1938 George Drew became leader of the Ontario Conservative Party. The Liberal Premier, Mitchell Hepburn, hated Mackenzie King with a hatred worthy of a Sicilian vendetta. On this Drew and he were not in disagreement, and his relations with Hepburn, who passed himself off as an "Ontario onion farmer" although he was a sophisticated political technician, were amiable.

In many ways George Drew was a political manager's dream. He had kept himself in the public eye for twenty-five years. His marriage to Fiorenza Johnson, daughter of the General Manager of the Metropolitan Opera, a lady of queenly distinction, was the social event of the decade.

An article by Drew in *Maclean's* magazine in 1938, "Canada's Armament Mystery", launched a public inquiry into the letting of armament contracts by the King government and led to the formation of a special purchasing department in the federal government.

The story had all the elements of classic intrigue. The John Inglis Company, inactive and on the verge of bankruptcy, had been awarded an exclusive contract to manufacture the versatile Czech machine gun, the Bren, for the Canadian Army. The head

99

of the company, a mysterious and romantic major named E. J. Hahn, was closely associated with various people in high places in the Liberal Party.

Into this atmosphere, a combination of E. Phillips Oppenheim and Ian Fleming, stepped George Drew, bringing light into the dark places of government intrigue and party patronage. In the spring of 1939, Drew appeared before the Public Accounts Committee of the House of Commons. In spite of his charges of political favouritism in the granting of the contract, he was kinder to Mackenzie King than might have been expected.

> I think Mr. Mackenzie King has shown the greatest possible desire that anyone could show to obtain the facts here and I am satisfied from the evidence and from his own departmental letters that if he had the slightest knowledge of the real pressure that was being brought to bear, that this contract would not have been signed.

(This was before Drew entered the field of federal politics. Once he did, moderation would give way to searing, savage attacks on the Grits.) In the outcome Drew's charges were more than vindicated, and he acquired a reputation for defending the public interest that was to grow with the years.

As Opposition Leader in the Ontario legislature in 1942, Drew again leaped to prominence by his fierce attack on the report of the Inquiry, headed by Sir Lyman Duff, into the capture of Canadian troops at Hong Kong. Drew charged that the report by the eminently respectable jurist was a whitewash of the government's stupidity and inefficiency in sending untrained and badly equipped troops to Hong Kong when they were fully aware that bastion of Empire was about to be taken by the Japanese. So seriously were Drew's charges regarded by the King government that Justice Minister Louis St. Laurent had Drew charged under the Defence of Canada Regulations as a menace to the war effort. St. Laurent withdrew the charges when Drew consented to modify his statements.

Drew became Premier of Ontario in 1943. In 1945 he won by a

landslide one week before Bracken went down to defeat in the federal election. By 1948 Drew was a national figure. Pierre Berton wrote in *Maclean's*:

> There are no unbiased opinions about Lieut. Col. George A. Drew, k.c., Premier of Ontario. He has been called conceited, arrogant, aloof, humorless, lovable, inspiring, dynamic and bashful.

In 1948 George Drew was again returned in Ontario. His capture of the French-speaking counties of eastern Ontario secured his claim to the Conservative national leadership at the 1948 Convention. The fact that the Drew administration, prior to the election, for the first time authorized, with considerable fanfare, a grant of some two hundred and fifty thousand dollars to the University of Ottawa was not entirely unrelated to the Conservative sweep in eastern Ontario.

Arriving in Ottawa for the 1948 leadership convention, Drew came on like a conquering hero, greeted by the kind of hyperbole usually reserved by the cynics in the Press Gallery for visiting movie stars.

"An Apollo Belvedere," one pundit exclaimed lyrically. George Drew at fifty-four was not quite that. Handsome, well set up, jovial, verging at times on pomposity on the platform, he had an air of being on parade which caused some editorial writers to refer to him by his militia title, Colonel Drew. They were not his friends. Hungry after thirteen years of exile from office, the Conservatives seized on Drew as a new Moses to lead them from Egyptian captivity.

I gave the keynote speech to the 1948 Convention at the Ottawa Coliseum, a kind of "cow palace" used for showing animals. I am not quite sure what I said; but no doubt there is a record in the press of the day. The convention began on September 30 and went on through October 1 and 2. There was a roar of applause when John Diefenbaker came in. I thought George Drew didn't have a chance. Little I knew. Alex Mackenzie, a renowned Ontario party organizer, sat beside me on the platform. "Don't worry," he said.

"Applause means nothing. It's in the bag for George." He told me exactly the number of votes by which Drew would carry the convention.

Diefenbaker was nominated by George Pearkes, a grand warrior, a major-general who had got into hot water with Mackenzie King by holding a press conference on the need for reinforcements during the conscription crisis. When Diefenbaker became Prime Minister, he made Pearkes Minister of National Defence and later Lieutenant-Governor of British Columbia.

I, of course, was for Drew. Like many others I regarded him as a winner, and it is true that he made of the Conservative parliamentary party a tightly knit fighting machine which was able to put the Liberals up against the wall in the 1956 Pipeline Debate.

Drew won a seat in the Carleton by-election in December 1948. His first Commons speech was not the set-piece exchange of formalities which the Liberals and some of the press expected. It was a slashing attack on the government's failure to mend its fences with the provinces, a powerful stand in favour of provincial rights, and a plea for returning taxing powers to the provinces where they belonged. Naturally this did not go down well with the centralizers in the St. Laurent government. Nor did it sit well with the friends of the Liberal Party in the Parliamentary Press Gallery.

Liberal strategy was to tar Drew with the provincial-rights brush, linking him with Maurice Duplessis as a threat to Confederation. Incidentally, as he recedes into the historical background, Duplessis, who was nothing if not a good Canadian and a gentleman — although I didn't agree with everything he stood for — begins to look a great deal better than some of those who bitterly attacked him in order to succeed him. Liberals like Jean Lesage, René Lévesque (a Liberal at the time), and even Robert Bourassa, have gone a great deal farther than Duplessis ever thought of going in straining the fabric of Confederation. Whatever else he might have been, Duplessis left no doubt in anyone's mind that he was a Canadian.

I once went to Montreal to speak against Duplessis's padlock law, which I described in the *Journal* as anti-democratic and unconstitutional. Duplessis never complained about that.

On the whole, my relations with Duplessis over many years, while not excessively cordial, were correct and friendly. He was appreciative of anything constructive the *Journal* said about him. In Ontario, which had not yet tasted the policies of Jean Lesage or of Lévesque's Parti Québécois, not to mention the F.L.Q. (a hobgoblin still hovering in the future), it was easy for the *Toronto Star* and other Liberal dailies to make Maurice Duplessis a thing of horror and a threat to all that was finest in the British heritage. He was, of course, no such thing; but newspaper nonsense is no respecter of persons or, for that matter, of truth.

Another one of the *Star's* nightmares, one whom they trotted out at election time with all the verve and spine-chilling panache of a performance of Grand Guignol, was Camillien Houde, the Mayor of Montreal, who at the outset of the war was sent to internment for advising French Canadians not to register for national service. It became the business of the *Star* and other purveyors of Liberal enlightenment (curiously today the *Star* isn't sure which side it's on, at least federally) to link George Drew with the machinations of the two Quebec bogeymen, Duplessis and Houde. I must say that Houde's appearance fitted the role the *Star* cast him in. He weighed in the neighbourhood of three hundred pounds, with a face that might be described as a cross between Pantagruel and the original Gargantua.

An example of the *Star's* tactics in the 1949 election drew my fire in a speech of welcome to George Drew before 7,000 people on a hot summer evening, the last night of the campaign, in the Ottawa Auditorium. This was the *Star's* front-page banner headline:

KEEP CANADA BRITISH

DESTROY DREW'S HOUDE

VOTE ST. LAURENT

For any newspaper to keep up any pretence of journalistic integrity after a performance of that kind was simple hypocrisy.

In my speech of introduction for Drew and his wife that night, I said:

The Toronto Star headline will, I hope, be repudiated by all responsible Canadians. To satisfy the political rancour and political fear of its publishers, the Star brought into its hymn of hate the name of the King, words dear throughout the Commonwealth and the Empire.

I called on Prime Minister St. Laurent to reject the *Star's* "dastardly act".

Every man who knows George Drew as a loyal heart in peace and war will punish through the sanction of the polls a thing as rancorous and indecent as this.

The *Star* was not, of course, the only offender in this respect. Liberal strategists dredged up every remark Drew had ever made, pored over his every saying, stayed up late trying to find ways of converting innocuous words into desecration of our most sacred institutions. Not all were as successful as the editorial staff of the *Star*, who must have stayed up a little later.

Someone discovered that Drew had once reminded French Canadians they were a conquered race, not a novel or a particularly endearing discovery. Jim Macdonnell and I worked very hard trying to get Drew to go into Quebec and discreetly admit his mistake. To no avail. He sometimes carried intransigence into personal relations, needlessly alienating Victor Sifton by a violent attack on his father. Although Victor had been best man at the Drews' wedding, George would not recant a single word.

Grant Dexter, in whom George Drew's Conservatism seemed to bring out the most violent Liberal reaction, coined the phrase the "Drew—Duplessis axis", which, of course, had all the evil connotations of the wartime Hitler—Mussolini—Tojo pact. Grant wrote article after article lining up Drew and Duplessis. A sample:

The Drew strategy consists in accepting in their entirety the policies of the Duplessis nationalist and isolated party of Quebec.

This was complete misrepresentation of both Drew and Duplessis; and I am wondering whether after all the advent of television has not made for more serious and responsible journalism. Such a statement, so wholly fabricated out of whole cloth, could not be made today. Drew did not accept, nor was he asked to, nor would he have been able to, since he didn't know what they were, all of the policies of the Duplessis party. And if that party was nationalist (since when has nationalism been a crime?), it certainly was not isolationist as far as the rest of Canada was concerned, although it may have been isolated, a clever use of a similar word. If Duplessis's party was isolated it was partly because the Liberals were in power in Ottawa and there was no welcome mat out for the Union Nationale leader.

In March 1949 Grant Dexter went so far as to admit that Drew had made an impression in Parliament; indeed that he was the "sensation of the session to date", welding a scattered party into a "hard-hitting, fighting force". This was nothing less than simple truth.

After the final Ottawa meeting in the 1949 campaign, when George spoke for over an hour in shirtsleeves and Fiorenza was charmingly brief in both English and French, I went back with them to the Roxborough. While George was in the kitchen getting drinks, she said, "What do you think?"

"He's going to be beaten badly."

"Don't tell George."

George was in ebullient humour, making plans for the composition of his new government and so on. I said nothing to disenchant him, finished my drink, and left.

I thought to myself, the Leader of the Opposition should have better accommodation than an apartment in the Roxborough. A few years later I managed to persuade J. W. McConnell, the sugar titan and publisher of the *Montreal Star*, the angel of my Gaspé campaign, to put up ten thousand dollars to purchase a residence for the Leader of the Opposition. A distinguished Liberal, Stanley McLean, organized a luncheon at the York Club and a group of tycoons provided thirty-five thousand. We bought Stornoway in Rockcliffe Park, a suburb of Ottawa.

Duncan MacTavish, a dedicated, goodhearted, and public-spirited Liberal, was a spark of the committee we set up, and I was happy to be on it. Stornoway cost forty thousand dollars to purchase from a daughter of Sir George Perley. That low figure was in itself a considerable contribution. Over the years we spent a hundred and seventy-five thousand to keep it up while it was tenanted by the St. Laurents, the Pearsons, the Diefenbakers, and the Stanfields. The responsibility has since been taken over by the federal government.

The day after I left the Drews in the Roxborough the Conservative Party was overwhelmed at the polls. St. Laurent came back with 190 seats to George Drew's 41,* a terrible blow to the man who had worked like a Trojan in the brief time allotted to him. Immediately he began to get ready for the next election.

It was inevitable that George Drew's chief opponent in the parliamentary battles of the next seven years should be, not Louis St. Laurent, but Clarence Decatur Howe. Howe, with his inflexibility, occasional arrogance, and iron determination, would have been the chief opponent of any Opposition leader who believed in democratic government. To George Drew, Howe was a red rag to a bull. More than once I felt, and George Drew himself felt, that in the knock-down battles between Drew and Howe, Louis St. Laurent's sympathies, motivated by strong democratic instincts, were on Drew's side.

In a series of bruising debates, the Defence Production Debate, the Canadair Debate, the Pipeline Debate, Drew cut the Liberal Party of Howe and St. Laurent and Walter Harris and Paul Martin down to size, so that, from a mere aspiration, victory became a definite possibility. Drew, ironically, was no longer in charge when it finally came.

C. D. Howe, an engineer, had made a formidable reputation during the war as Minister of Munitions and Supply. As a result of the Bren Gun Inquiry military purchasing had been placed under Howe, and this was the genesis of the Department of Munitions and Supply. On a wartime visit to England, Howe's ship was torpedoed and the indestructible minister spent eight hours in an open boat. By the end of the war Howe was above criticism, an untouchable of government, a man who got things done, a man who could do no wrong.

---

*(1949) Liberal 190, Progressive Conservative 41, C.C.F. 13, Social Credit 10, Others 8. In 1945 the Liberals had won 125 seats and the Conservatives 67.

In 1948 Howe became Minister of Trade and Commerce and in 1951 he took on the additional portfolio of Defence Production. The first crack in the façade of his power came in debate on a government motion to perpetuate wartime powers in the Defence Production Act. Howe did not help matters by refusing to make the slightest concession to Opposition demands. In an attempt to curb the appetite of a government too long in power, the Opposition mounted a filibuster. George Drew, with his corporal's guard of fifty Conservatives, determined to hold up the plans of the ambitious minister.

For two weeks the battle raged. Each day Howe came in, craggy-faced, granite-voiced, stonewalling all Opposition demands for a watering down of his powers to meet changing peacetime conditions. The Opposition tore into the bill like dogs worrying a bone while Howe sat there, his heavy eyebrows standing out on his beet-red face. Drew led the fight against the amended bill, aided by the Commons experience of M. J. Coldwell and by Stanley Knowles's knowledge of Commons rules and procedures. Behind Drew were Howard Green, tall, reedy-voiced, a model of rectitude; Gordon Graydon, a smiling bulldog; Donald Fleming, filled with anger at the usurpations of Howe. Drew's booming voice filled the Chamber day after day; at one point he stayed on his feet for eight hours with a short break for dinner.

Howe finally got fed up and went off to Sept Iles on a fishing trip, leaving St. Laurent to handle the situation. One afternoon I got a call from Drew. He asked me to meet him at the Rideau Club. In the upstairs lounge, with its leather chairs and portraits of Macdonald and Laurier, he told me he'd had a strange phone call from Louis St. Laurent offering to water down the bill to meet the demands of the Opposition. He didn't know what to make of it.

Of course, what the Opposition wanted was for the Department to continue in existence but for the special powers of the minister to come to an end, leaving Howe with the same status as any other minister in the government. St. Laurent seemed agreeable, but Drew couldn't believe he would do a thing like this to Howe, brave Howe's anger, even though he was Prime Minster.

However, St. Laurent seemed quite determined and quite sincere. He said he would work on the bill on the weekend at St.

Patrice and would provide Drew with a revised draft on Monday. I went down to Stornoway on Monday for lunch. At 12:45 St. Laurent phoned as agreed and Drew had me on the extension. St. Laurent quickly read over his revisions, which met the suggestions Drew had made to him in every respect. He promised the revised bill would be on Drew's desk when the House met.

It was the first time I had seen Drew baffled. "What can I do? We'll have to put it through. I can't even tell my caucus much less the press what's happened. What the hell is St. Laurent up to?"

"He's a corporation lawyer," I suggested. "He's getting the best settlement he can. Out of court."

True to his word, St. Laurent had the new bill on Drew's desk at two o'clock. That ended the filibuster. I think Drew was a little disappointed. He enjoyed hammering away at the government. To be very frank about it, had it not been for C. D. Howe Drew's task would have been immeasurably more difficult.

Personally, I enjoyed C.D., and when I happened to be playing golf with him some time later, I asked: "Did you know when you went away that St. Laurent was going to pull your bill out from under you?"

"Like hell I did." Although Howe had a certain admiration for St. Laurent, the relationship was very different from that with Mackenzie King. "King never interfered," C.D. told me. "He let me have my head. He didn't know a damn thing about business or industry. Didn't really give a damn. But St. Laurent, with his experience as a corporation lawyer, is always one jump ahead. He knows exactly what's going on. You never have to spell things out. This is good in some ways. But "—C.D. paused to address his ball, sighting down the long, green fairway at St. Andrews — "you can't put anything over on the bugger." That was C.D. —tough, sometimes crude, absolutely honest, a great engineer and builder, laughable as a House of Commons man.

All of this was, of course, preliminary to what has become known as the Great Pipeline Debate, which constituted a definite and serious reversal to twenty years of unchallenged Liberal supremacy. There are still "Liberals" who say they are unable to see why the Pipeline Debate should have constituted a major national issue. In a party which had begun to believe itself infallible and untouchable, that attitude is easy to understand. Therein, of course, lies the danger in prolonged power: that the unthinkable becomes normal.

It was unthinkable that a minister should walk into the House with a measure of national importance and say before debate had even begun that a time limit would be imposed on each phase of the discussion. When C. D. Howe was the minister and the government was the aging and jaded government left by Mackenzie King to Louis St. Laurent, the unthinkable became the inevitable.

The Pipeline Debate unmasked the arrogance of twenty years of uninterrupted Liberal power. The Defence Production Debate had taught the Opposition that the government could be stopped; it taught C. D. Howe that the Opposition must be given no opportunity to filibuster and obstruct. Howe's intransigence and Drew's determination met head on.

Howe committed the government and people of Canada to some $80 million in the form of guaranteed loans to American builders of a pipeline carrying gas from Alberta to eastern Canada, a distance of 3,000 miles.

Howe made the mistake on the first day of the debate of telling the House the debate would be shut off by closure. He left the Opposition no choice but to take a stand. First and foremost, Howe's intransigence and contempt of Parliament, if not opposed, meant that life as a parliamentarian simply would not be worth living. Parliament would be reduced to vassalage. Secondly, members on all sides of the House, and more particularly in the Conservative and c.c.f. parties, were appalled at the idea of lending public money to an American-owned firm to construct a Canadian utility.

The notion of limiting the debate because of an undertaking given by Howe to the pipeline promoters was equally galling. When someone is prepared to go to inordinate lengths to achieve an objective, the House is always suspicious. Howe knew this, or should have known. He wanted the line through by a certain date and the bill was going through the House come hell or high water. His associates with parliamentary experience let him down.

Howe was thus placed in a position to learn what others learned before him and others have yet to learn: Parliament can be led but never driven. In this connection, one of the most successful House Leaders the Liberals ever had was George McIlraith, who got measures through by appearing completely uninterested.

Of course, Howe's personal prestige was at stake. The Opposition sensed this; against Howe's prestige they pitted the prestige of Parliament. It was a contest Howe could not win; he won the bill and lost the issue by proving that Opposition charges of Liberal arrogance and contempt of Parliament were more than mere sloganeering. In the process, the government subjected itself to wounds from which it was unable to recover.

As the debate degenerated into a slogging match, with Howe remorselessly closing off each phase with a closure motion, the temper of the House deteriorated. The government showed signs of cracking under pressure when Walter Harris, the House Leader, was accused of sending a note to Speaker René Beaudoin. From two episodes Walter Harris's political career never recovered: one occurred while he was Minister of Immigration when he granted landed-immigrant status to the labour thug Hal Banks; the other was his involvement at C. D. Howe's side in the Pipeline Debate.

One of the regrettable aspects of the affair was the destruction of the Speaker, René Beaudoin, for being too loyal to his party and not faithful enough to his oath as Speaker. Beaudoin was under tremendous pressure, attested to by the lineup of Cabinet ministers' limousines in front of his house. As the debate wore on, his customary urbanity was replaced by an anxious frown.

Sittings went on until the small hours of the morning. Donald Fleming was named by the Speaker and left the Chamber; his desk was draped by his colleagues with a Union Jack.

When C.C.F. member Colin Cameron raised a question of privilege based on a letter critical of Beaudoin in an Ottawa newspaper, Beaudoin allowed himself to be led into a discussion that lasted two and a half hours, and the House adjourned without the usual closure motion being put. Howe was furious. A new closure motion was required with advance notice of twenty-four hours, which, in view of the approaching weekend, meant that

Howe could not meet his deadline for getting the bill through.

A decision had to be made. The choice lay between throwing either Howe or Beaudoin to the lions, and Beaudoin lost. When the House opened the next day—quickly given the rather melo-dramatic description "Black Friday" — Beaudoin rose and ad-vanced the incredible proposal that the House should wipe out the previous day's proceedings, reverting to where matters stood be-fore the question of privilege was raised. Pandemonium broke loose. George Drew stormed red-faced into the aisle. M. J. Cold-well, c.c.f. leader and mildest of men, waved a fist at the Speaker from the bottom of the table. Drew moved a motion of censure against Beaudoin which was defeated. Howe got his bill through but the government suffered a setback which was to bring defeat in the next election. René Beaudoin ended his days as a bartender in Arizona, a victim of the mythology that a Liberal government could do no wrong.

By shattering that myth the Pipeline Debate cost the Liberal Party dearly. Public opinion hardened against the government. For a time the Liberal Party lost the allegiance of its most faithful interpreter, Grant Dexter, who was appalled and disgusted by the whole performance. The Pipeline Debate was a watershed. It re-vealed the arrogance and intemperance of power too long retained and too little accounted for; it revealed the encrustation of age and arterial degeneration by which the government was affected.

The Pipeline Debate was a textbook example of a breakdown of the parliamentary process because of undue pressures placed on it by the governing party. While the House was in the throes of the debate I wrote about the parliamentary principles involved.

Mr. Howe gave notice of closure in Parliament before the Opposition had an opportunity to say as much as a word on his Trans-Canada Pipeline Resolution.

This is not closure in the sense of closure being used to defeat obstruction and permit orderly and necessary Parliamentary proce-dure; it is perversion and abuse of closure. The gag, the guillotine, pure and simple.

Closure first came to Britain's Parliament when Parnell and Biggar, inventors and masters of obstruction, attempted to make Irish Home Rule the price of Parliament proceeding at all. That was in the 1880's and since then closure has been applied at Westminster not to curb reasonable debate but only to ensure that the House complete the legislative program within reasonable time.

I went on to review closure in the Canadian Parliament: Sir Robert Borden's Naval Aid Bill, the bill guaranteeing Canadian National Railway bonds, the Wartime Elections Act, and other instances in 1926 and 1932. I placed the responsibility for the current crisis at the door of Louis St. Laurent:

> Mr. Howe is being blamed for this; called a dictator. Yet the truth is that Mr. Howe is no more to blame than any of his colleagues, this unprecedented method of applying closure representing clearly a planned tactic by the entire Cabinet.
>
> And not the least extraordinary thing about the whole business is that closure on this Trans Canada Pipeline transaction is being imposed, with debate emasculated, without the Prime Minister having deigned to explain or defend the proposition by a single word.

On May 29, 1956, I asked:

> What is the source, the underlying cause of those ugly scenes in Parliament?
>
> The source is not alone in the character of the Government's pipeline legislation, largely the creature of the Trans Canada Pipeline Company's repeated failures and broken promises, nor in the Government's double-talk and broken promises to the House. It is more and fundamentally in the Government's determination to force the result of such combined wrongness through Parliament by a process of closure unknown to British legislatures—a process which the Liberal Winnipeg Free Press calls "an abomination to the heart of every man of every party who cares for free discussion and democratic institutions".

I then turned to what was happening to the institution of

15. At work, 1959.

16 & 17. (*Above left*) A retirement gift for a longtime friend and colleague, Tommy Lowrey. (*Right*) Chairman, Royal Commission on Publications, 1961.

18 & 19. (*Opposite page, above*) I. Norman Smith, O'Leary's successor as Editor and President of the *Ottawa Journal*. (*Below*) a Beaton cartoon for September 7, 1961.

"TIME, ANYONE?"

20 & 21. (*Above*) George Drew. (*Below*) John G. Diefenbaker.

22 & 23. (*Above*) Robert L. Stanfield. (*Below*) With Ontario Premier John Robarts.

24 & 25. At the testimonial dinner for Grattan O'Leary held in the
Parliament Buildings, Ottawa, on June 18, 1975, Prime Minister Pierre
Trudeau congratulates the guest of honour, with Earl Rowe looking on.
(*Right*) In his Senate office, September 1974.

Newspaper Hall of Fame
1967

Senator M. Grattan O'Leary

Newspaper ink has flowed through the veins of Senator O'Leary for more than half a century. Confidant of Prime Ministers and in the inner circle of Canadian politics for years, he combines eloquence of speech and facility of pen in pungent defence of his ideals. In this Centennial Year, he remains one of the most notable Canadian newspaper men since Confederation.

His election was made by the News Hall of Fame Committee of the Toronto Men's Press Club.

Arthur L. Cole.
Chairman, News Hall of Fame
Committee

O.S.O. Mason
President, Toronto Men's
Press Club

Speaker under René Beaudoin and the pressure he was being
subjected to by the government.

> The Chair, the Speaker is the very soul of Parliament; without faith in
> the Speaker's rulings, without confidence in his impartiality and
> integrity, with fear that the Speaker has become just another mes-
> senger of the House doing the bidding of men who happen to be on the
> Treasury benches, Parliament becomes nothing.

I went on to say:

> That is why we have had these ugly scenes in Parliament; why Mr.
> Fleming, fighting desperately to have his rights as a member re-
> spected, defied a ruling of the Deputy Speaker and was suspended. The
> Opposition, being rode roughshod by Mr. Howe and Mr. Harris (the
> Prime Minister who should be the real leader of the House not heard
> from) has been driven to tactics of defiance.

I am often amused by the convention that newspaper comment
must be bland and innocuous, not to say gelatinous; carefully
conjured so as neither to give nor to invite offence. What men like
P. D. Ross or John W. Dafoe or Grant Dexter would have made of
that theory is best left to the imagination. A healthy strain of
irritability is almost necessary for a good editorial writer. If he
cannot get worked up over his subject then he is better to take up
some less robust vocation.

I felt sorry for Louis St. Laurent, a good and decent man, a
democrat at heart, no longer able to control his party. The Pipeline
Debate offended his every instinct; he patently and obviously
made his withdrawal plain by burying his face in, of all things,
Good Housekeeping magazine.

Of all the faces and personalities which stand out, from Laurier
to Trudeau, Louis St. Laurent was worthy to rank with any. The
pipeline fiasco, I am sure, was a sickening experience for this
chivalrous and debonair frequenter of the nation's board rooms.
Howe demanded a free hand and St. Laurent let him have it. That
was his mistake. It was the Prime Minister's duty to see that the

use of closure was not abused. I really believe myself that C. D. Howe didn't know how to use closure. He didn't understand it. He was depending on Walter Harris and Jack Pickersgill.

St. Laurent liked George Drew. Occasionally after Sunday mass he would drop in at Stornoway for late breakfast. Part French, part Irish, something in St. Laurent responded to the fighter in Drew. I am sure St. Laurent would not have been greatly disturbed if George Drew had been Prime Minister of Canada.

When Drew became ill in the months following the Pipeline Debate, St. Laurent said to me, "I want to do something for George. If he should have to give up on account of his health, I want to name him High Commissioner to London." The offer was sincere and well meant, with no ulterior motive but to set Drew's mind at ease. At that moment Drew was a very ill man, far more so than he realized or would admit. At one point when Drew's health took a turn for the worse, St. Laurent called him personally and said, "George, I want you to work hard at your recovery. I would like very much to send you on an important assignment to London." Such was the breadth of St. Laurent's innate decency and honour.

The tincture of tragedy that marred George Drew's career was evident in the serious and lingering illness that struck him down at a time when it appeared his hold on the party leadership was strong and secure. He had fought two elections against Louis St. Laurent, who was obviously tiring, and in 1953 had come back with ten seats more than in 1949.* Not a spectacular result but one calculated to give some hope for the next election, which would probably take place in 1957.

Following the pipeline disaster, Drew was full of confidence in his ability to lead the party to victory. Equally important, the party was full of confidence in Drew. The dogs of dissension, which appear to spend a great deal of time barking at the heels of the Conservative Party, were mercifully silent, if only for a time, and it looked as though everything was coming up roses for

* (1953) Liberal 170, Progressive Conservative 51, C.C.F. 23, Social Credit 15, Others 6.

George Drew when he was laid low by a combination of accumulated fatigue and a virus infection very difficult to pinpoint and deal with.

Drew's medical advisers decided, no doubt wisely, that the pressure and fatigue of the leadership had to be forgone in order to bring Drew back to health. Fiorenza knew but George did not. Who was to have the unenviable task of telling him? I was asked, along with Léon Balcer, who was president of the National Association, and Jim Macdonnell, to see Dr. Ray Farquharson, a personal friend of Drew's and his physician. Farquharson did not mince words.

"Either he retires or you gentlemen will soon be attending his funeral." There was no gainsaying the ominousness of those words. We were, of course, thunderstruck. George had been doing marvellously well in the House. We knew, of course, he'd had a bout of meningitis. We now discovered he'd gone back to work far too soon, pooh-poohing the efforts of the medical people to get him to take care of himself. Now he was tired and run down and not improving the way he should. Farquharson brought in a second specialist, who confirmed the verdict. "He's got to get out of politics or you had better prepare for the worst."

We met with Earl Rowe, a pillar of strength in the party and an old friend and mentor of George's, and we came to the decision that the only way to make George look after himself was to draft a letter and bring it to his sickbed for his signature. Fiorenza, who at this point was very anxious about George, pleaded with him to do as the doctors asked.

At first George would have nothing to do with it. Storm in a teacup. He would be up and about in a week or two. Finally Fiorenza managed to convince him it was for his own good. Looking as though he couldn't believe it himself he signed the letter of resignation and I took it away. I wasn't too surprised when I got back to my room in the Royal York and there was a phone call from George. "Look, Grattan, it's all nonsense. I'm fit as a fiddle."

"What do you want me to do, George?"

"I'm withdrawing the letter."

"You can't do it, George." I gave it to him from the shoulder —

115

what Fiorenza hadn't dared tell him. "The doctor says you'll be dead in six months if you don't get out."

There was a long silence. "All right," George said.

Any suggestion that the party kicked out George Drew or wanted him to leave is sheer nonsense. The party would have gone with George Drew to the gates of hell and back. He represented the very best type of Conservative thinking. A man who knew what he believed and where he stood on the issues. After a succession of leaders like Hanson and Bracken and Manion, Drew was manna in the desert. An outstanding parliamentarian, he would have made an excellent Prime Minister. He left a tightly knit organization in contrast to the disarray which existed when he took over the reins of the party.

Louis St. Laurent, regrettably, was not enabled to fulfil his desire to name George Drew High Commissioner in London. This, along with other unfinished business of the St. Laurent government, like firing James E. Coyne and cancelling the Arrow, was left for the victor in the 1957 election, John G. Diefenbaker.

I am sure that had he won the 1957 election, Mr. St. Laurent would have done everything he intended to do. He was a man of honour, supreme balance, and utter realism. He was not the kind of person one could easily get close to. And yet I recall an extraordinary interview just before he became Prime Minister, when he was still Secretary of State for External Affairs and living at the Roxborough, that Dowager Empress of Ottawa apartment buildings, since torn down.

Maclean's wanted an intimate profile of St. Laurent. He agreed, and on a Sunday evening I presented myself just at eight o'clock. St. Laurent was alone in an apartment neither large nor distinguished. We sat down and he gave me a drink and told me he had just come from seeing Sir Lyman Duff, retired Chief Justice of the Supreme Court of Canada, laden with years and honours in the law.

"This may surprise you, O'Leary. I asked for his advice on whether to stay in politics or go back to the law."

"I can guess what he told you."

"You're right. He told me to get out. Can you guess what my decision will be?"

116

"I think you'll stay."

He laughed. Sir Lyman had strongly advised him to return to his corporation law practice. Young lawyers were coming up, and regardless of how big a name a man had, once he lost touch it was hard to pick up the pieces. I thought this was rather good advice.

St. Laurent gave his famous shrug and said, "I'll be very frank. I am not too happy with Quebec's representation in the government." I could see St. Laurent's point. Ernest Bertrand, Roch Pinard, Hugues Lapointe, Alcide Côté, and even Jean Lesage were nice people but hardly the type to decide a nation's destiny.

I brought up the question of Mackenzie King's intentions. Surely he would retire soon. St. Laurent made a pooh-poohing expression. "Those stories about Mr. King's retirement must be taken with a grain of salt. We have been hearing them for a long time. Mr. King is not a man to retire.

"You know," he said, "You might say that I am an accidental Liberal. I never knew Laurier, although I once shook his hand, a supreme moment. I started out in a Conservative firm. Our senior partner was Pelletier, Borden's Postmaster General. One day I was told it would be a good idea to take an interest in the Liberal Party, attend meetings, show my face, help to dispel the idea that everyone in the firm was a *bleu*." This went on for some years with St. Laurent maintaining a tenuous connection with the Liberal Party but infinitely more interested in practising law, when all of a sudden out of the night came the phone call from King offering him a position in the Cabinet, the sort of thing you wouldn't believe if you saw it in a television play.

A good Catholic, he delayed his answer while he went and consulted Cardinal Villeneuve, who told him that for the sake of Quebec he must accept. "As you know, O'Leary, I am in a strange position with an Irish mother and French-Canadian father. I feel it helps me to understand both viewpoints. Like yourself, I feel it is possible to be a good Irishman and a good Quebecer at the same time." That was a shrewd shot, because hadn't I been practising it all my life, myself?

He pointed out that a French Canadian at the federal level was always under pressure, as Laurier was under pressure from the Quebec bishops on the Manitoba schools question. "I want to

117

show you something." He went to a writing desk in the corner and drew out a letter bearing the episcopal seal of the Archbishop of Montreal. My French was just good enough with his assistance to make out that the letter was a strong argument from Archbishop Charbonneau in favour of admitting Franco Spain to the United Nations. St. Laurent had opposed the resolution on behalf of Canada.

Well, of course, Charbonneau was the bishop who, within a short while, was turfed out of Quebec by Duplessis for taking up a collection in Montreal parishes in aid of striking asbestos workers. He ended his days in a convent in Victoria, a sort of French-Canadian Cardinal Mindszenty.

Our chat whiled away the evening hours. St. Laurent imposed no conditions about what I might use or not use — no nonsense about "off the record" remarks, no coyness of that sort. He spoke almost as though he wanted to unburden himself, so that at least one representative of the press in Ottawa would know how he felt about things.*

It has always been a principle of mine to respect the confidences of those I interviewed, even when not asked. I have not willingly or deliberately written things that I knew would harm others unless, of course, the public interest demanded it. This is not pure altruism: in journalism respect for the rights of others ensures greater longevity.

* It was during this interview that Mr. St. Laurent gave me the account of the conscription crisis that is recorded earlier (p. 90-2).

DIEFENBAKER

In 1956 the Conservative Party was once again without a leader. Since 1919 we had had six, the Liberals two. St. Laurent had soundly beaten the Conservatives under George Drew in two national elections and there seemed no reason why he shouldn't do the same at least once more against any leader the Conservatives were capable of putting up.

The prospects were not too bright. George Nowlan went to see Sidney Smith at the University of Toronto; he wasn't having any. Who could blame him? What attraction was there in an out-of-office party of fifty members? Against Louis St. Laurent and his old-world, avuncular charm, there did not seem any likelihood of the Conservatives' taking office in the foreseeable future.

There was no French Canadian available of national stature. Conservative candidates in the Province of Quebec were still running against Wilfrid Laurier. In the West there were Howard Green and Davie Fulton, and in Ontario there was Donald Fleming. Leslie Frost wouldn't touch the leadership with a ten-foot pole; besides, we didn't want to follow an Ontario premier with another Ontario premier.

There was always Diefenbaker. The man from Saskatchewan had a spotty record as a long-time loser in the politics of that province. He'd been a good M.P. and made a reputation by forcing issues and by his evangelical way of speaking. A born crusader, he had tried for the leadership in 1942 and again in 1948. He wanted it badly. The trouble was the party didn't want Diefenbaker.

Diefenbaker was erratic. No one knew what he was going to do. It was a question whether he knew himself. He was politically unreliable, sometimes with the party, at other times, as on family allowances, voting against the party and with the government. That kind of thing does not endear a candidate to party managers. There was some doubt whether Diefenbaker was really a Conservative; he was a bit too much the western radical for the eastern establishment of the party. After the experience with Bracken the party was not keen on another political virgin from the West, particularly one with Diefenbaker's messianic, apocryphal approach, far too reminiscent at times of R. B. Bennett. We did not want another man of destiny.

Under Drew's leadership Diefenbaker seemed to go into eclipse. He hadn't done much in the Pipeline Debate, letting Drew, Fleming, Howard Green, and Fulton carry the fight.

Diefenbaker was just as liable to forget about the issues before the House and go haring off after one of his pet crusades — the need for a Bill of Rights, suspension of habeas corpus in the Gouzenko spy arrests, government by Order-in-Council, and so on. Not the material of which election victories are made.

We had the convention in December 1956 and Diefenbaker walked away with it, swamping Donald Fleming and Davie Fulton. The Quebec delegates, who wanted Fleming, walked out of the hall led by Léon Balcer, a bad augury for Diefenbaker's future as leader.

In April 1957 Parliament was dissolved and an election was called for June 10. Diefenbaker capitalized on Liberal complacency, inertia, and ineptness to launch a whirlwind campaign across the country, ramming home heavily the lesson of Liberal arrogance underscored in the Pipeline Debate. The Liberals, grown weary in office, helped.

C. D. Howe got into an unlovely public slanging match with a group of wheat farmers, and a youth was flung down from the platform at one of St. Laurent's meetings, rather putting paid to the "Uncle Louis" image. Instead, St. Laurent emerged in the merciless eye of the television cameras, which were covering a national election for the first time, as old, tired, and more than a little testy.

When the election ended, Diefenbaker, to everyone's surprise, perhaps even his own, was Prime Minister of Canada.* At the head of a minority government made up of those who had opposed his leadership as well as those who supported him, he drove through measures bringing aid to the aged, the poor, the farmers, and others in a society neglected under a Liberalism grown fat in office.

Lester Pearson, who had made his name as Minister for External Affairs with the help of loyal friends in the Press Gallery, had the unenviable task of bringing to an exhausted Louis St. Laurent the news that the party felt he was no longer capable of leading it.

In January 1958 Pearson was chosen to take over the wobbling Liberal forces. In a fatuous move now attributed to Jack Pickersgill's advice, Pearson came fresh from the convention, Nobel Peace Prize in hand, and replaced the peace prize with a dunce cap when he rose in the House and suggested Diefenbaker should resign and let him take over.

This performance, of a kind more suited to the Common Room than to the Commons, won Pearson a merciless dressing down from Diefenbaker, who proceeded to call an unheard-of March election and roll up a total of 208 seats, 50 of them in Quebec,† partly through the good offices of Maurice Duplessis, who for the first time personally intervened in a federal campaign.

With the largest majority in Canadian history, John Diefenbaker proceeded to antagonize the British, the Americans, a considerable part of the public service, his own members (particularly those from Quebec), the Press Gallery, and finally the Conservative Party itself. This cumulative alienation did not take place overnight. It took time. But by the time Diefenbaker went to the country in June 1962 the situation was such that his enormous

---

*(1957) Progressive Conservative 112, Liberal 105, C.C.F. 25, Social Credit 19, Others 4. This was a loss of 65 seats for the Liberals, and a gain of 61 for the Conservatives.

†(1958) Progressive Conservative 208, Liberal 48, C.C.F. 8, Others 1.

backlog of 208 seats melted down to a bare 116.* It had required only four years of power to reduce the Diefenbaker government from a record majority back to a minority position.

I had not been a Diefenbaker supporter from the beginning. But I recognized his bulldog capacity to worry an issue until he won his point, his speaking ability, his feeling for the little man. An outstanding criminal lawyer, he made his reputation fighting for the underdog. He was never an easy man to be with or to talk to. His impatience with the views of others, the pressures he was under, made it extremely difficult to be relaxed in his presence.

I saw quite a bit of him in the early stages. I wrote speeches for him. When he went to Ireland I gave him notes for the North and for the South; and of course he mixed them up and delivered the notes intended for the North in Dublin and the notes intended for the South in Belfast. When General de Gaulle came in April 1960 Diefenbaker asked me to prepare some notes and I gladly did so. I did the same for John Kennedy's visit to Canada in May 1961. When Diefenbaker delivered his attack on Khrushchev at the United Nations in September 1960 I contributed to the peroration, borrowing the phrase "death's pale flag" from *Romeo and Juliet*, and dictating for half an hour over the phone from Ottawa to Diefenbaker's secretary, Bunny Pound, in New York. I used the lines in a similar passage a few years later in a speech to a group of American congressmen in Houston.

In September 1962, although I never asked for anything, Diefenbaker made me a Senator. I shall always feel that this was not a personal gesture but recognition on behalf of the party for years of active service.

Speaking in the Senate on December 11, 1968, on the question of where a Senator's loyalty should lie, I made my position very plain, both as a Senator and as a supporter of the Conservative Party, the party of Borden, Meighen, and Bennett, a party too historic and too great in its contribution to become identified with the political fortunes of a single individual.

*(1962) Progressive Conservative 116, Liberal 99, Social Credit 30, N.D.P.19, Others 1.

I have heard honourable Senators in this House, and I have regretted hearing it, say how grateful they were to the Prime Minister who appointed them. Well, Honourable Senators, I never felt any gratitude to the Prime Minister who appointed me. I did not say, "You can have my conscience if you will send me to the Senate." I believe and I have acted accordingly, that my job here is to apply my Conservative philosophy to the consideration of the legislation coming to us in this house, but accepting the Conservative philosophy is to me a very different thing from accepting the Conservative Party line.

Such was my view then. Such is my view now. I was very well treated by my new colleagues and I was favourably impressed with the warmth, humanity, and intelligence of the place, a feeling which has never left.

I had said in my maiden speech on October 17, 1962, that I was there not as a political eunuch but as a partisan of the Conservative Party. I took exception to a remark by the government leader, the Honourable Ross Macdonald, to the effect that legislation coming from the government must be subjected to particularly careful scrutiny because it was a minority government.

Why all this wonderment, all this amazement about what is called minority government? There is nothing strange, nothing new, nothing mysterious about minority government. In the very fatherland of Parliamentary Government they have had minority governments again and again. Mr. Pitt governed England for many years; he never had an organized parliamentary majority behind him. In the 1890's Mr. Gladstone had two governments that were in a minority, actually dependent on the Irish nationalists of Mr. Parnell.

So much for the uses of history. The Senators did not appear to resent being beaten over the head with Mr. Pitt and Mr. Gladstone in my first Senate appearance, an indication of the wise tolerance and sophistication of the institution.

Well, of course, in that first speech I had to get into the Common Market and the impact on Canadian trade of Britain's proposed entry, which I regarded as something inevitable to which we might as well resign ourselves. I defended the Prime Minister's position in this respect against those who were attacking him. Certain London journals charged that in his stand on the Common Market Diefenbaker was speaking on behalf of "yokels on the Prairies" and I pointed out that the yokels were good enough to go to England's rescue in two wars.

I touched on the devaluation issue. I was not shocked or scandalized by the fact the Diefenbaker government found it necessary to devalue the dollar. Anyone who knew a bit of history would have realized it was a sign that Canadians were too prosperous and were spending too much. I recalled that when D. C. Abbott devalued the dollar on behalf of the King government the whole operation was conducted by radio and no one thought anything of it.

On the Diefenbaker government's record as a whole I said:

> When I look at the program of the government I am truly amazed at what they have been able to do. However, my amazement is almost equal when I see how little they have been able to accomplish in telling the public what they have done. This is one of the most curious things about this government. Active in every way, vigorous in every way, they seem to have been completely inarticulate when they came to telling the people of Canada just what they had done.

Following the 1962 election, more a defeat than a victory, Diefenbaker attempted to pick up the scattered pieces of his power. He made some changes in the Cabinet, bringing in, as Minister of Trade and Commerce, Wallace McCutcheon, who continued to sit in the Senate. A man of tremendous personal prestige, McCutcheon was a financial leader, a close associate of E. P. Taylor in the giant Argus Corporation; his job was to impose financial stability and restore the confidence of investors. He was there to represent the financial hierarchy in Toronto.

The shaky Diefenbaker government immediately became plagued by internal dissension under a Prime Minister who didn't seem to be able to make up his mind. Parliament was not summoned until fall, allowing precious months to slip by while the government dithered.

During the summer of 1962 Diefenbaker gave the appearance of a man harassed beyond endurance. Grey, shaken, he appeared to be losing command of himself and his government. When Parliament opened he seemed to recover some of his power; but it was not long before the Cuban crisis showed a government still incapable of reaching decisions on matters of life and death. This was especially galling to Douglas Harkness, who expressed his disgust to me and others in various conversations. A particularly aggravating point for Harkness, as Minister of National Defence, was the delay in the acquisition of the nuclear warheads that would make the Bomarc missiles and Starfighter jets already acquired by Canada effective. Despite a commitment to its allies the government could not make up its mind on this decisive step that would make the weapons operational.

In January 1963 a dramatic turnabout by Lester Pearson and the Liberal Party on the question of nuclear armament meant there could be no further postponement on the issue. Pearson said that the warheads should be acquired in fulfilment of Canada's commitment and that a Liberal government would do so, later negotiating a release from the commitment.

Still the government refused to decide. On January 30, 1963, as the Canadian Cabinet was meeting to discuss the nuclear issue, the American State Department, by way of a press release, let loose an unprecedented broadside in which it contradicted statements made by the Prime Minister in the House. There is no question that the action harmed the Diefenbaker government and helped to weaken it immeasurably on the eve of its defeat. The *Ottawa Journal* said in its lead editorial on February 1:

> There was not one party leader in the House of Commons yesterday who defended the methods used by the State Department. That measure of the indignation felt by Canadians is the most alarming development of all. . . .
>
> They must be laughing in Moscow today. General Charles de Gaulle who likes to think of President Kennedy as a menace to smaller countries, must be laughing today. . . .
>
> And what was Washington thinking of when it believed that thus to attack the Canadian Government would better Washington's chances

of winning broad Canadian support for nuclear warheads? . . .

Pearson's stand was certainly in line with what the Americans wanted; and there is no question that Kennedy badly wanted Diefenbaker to be beaten, as clearly shown in Sorensen's book *Kennedy*. The direct intervention of the State Department in the crisis, allegedly without Kennedy's knowledge, is sufficient indication of where the American government stood.

Diefenbaker, who had been depressed, almost distraught, through the summer, was now back on top, convinced in his own mind that, with the American intervention, he had a winning issue, and determined to take the party and the country with him. This revival of buoyancy in the Prime Minister as the country swept on on a collision course with the United States had something fateful and ominous about it.

As Diefenbaker rushed into headlong confrontation with the Americans over the nuclear issue, this man who failed to understand the meaning of compromise again threw near-panic into the financial community. Canada was on the verge of economic recovery after four years of high unemployment and falling production; the last thing the nation needed was a nasty confrontation with the United States. And this is just what Diefenbaker was determined to achieve.

As in an old-time movie, tension mounted, that tension Diefenbaker loved so dearly to generate; but if his glands required the excitement of being strapped to a plank while the giant buzz-saw screamed nearer and nearer, there were thousands of Canadians who had no desire to be strapped on the plank with him. They did not share Diefenbaker's confidence that rescue would take place at the last minute. Nor, of course, did they have the advantage of reading—and even writing—the script.

In his own Cabinet and party the tension produced wide and deep cleavages; restlessness grew in caucus as Diefenbaker seemed determined to lead the party to new catastrophes. This time the country itself could be seriously affected in its defence relationship with our major ally, the United States. Certainly it was hard for most Canadians, including Conservative M.P.'s, to buy the picture of John Kennedy presented by Diefenbaker. That this most literate and articulate of Presidents could be the monster Diefenbaker painted him surpassed the powers of imagination. McCutcheon was increasingly perturbed at the direction events were taking. In his estimation, Diefenbaker's course led to untold damage in our relations with the United States. The Americans were not going to be pushed around in order to advance the political ambitions of the Canadian Prime Minister.

Others who had fought the good fight for the Conservative Party when there weren't any rewards for doing so—men like Jim Macdonnell, who had stood with Gordon Graydon and Earl Rowe and George Drew against the panoplied might of Liberal power; like George Nowlan, who knew what the Conservative Party was about, knew it not as an aggregation of radical demagogues but as a party with a history and a past, a party with responsibility for its actions and policies; like Davie Fulton, who did not believe that elections must be won at any price, regardless of the future cost to the country and the party—were increasingly disturbed.

People like Léon Balcer, a former National President, faithful to the party over the years, discerned no place for French Canada in Diefenbaker's calculations.

The showdown came when Douglas Harkness, the Minister of National Defence, came to the conclusion that the Prime Minister had no intention of acquiring the warheads, leaving Harkness no alternative but to resign.

At this point, George Nowlan, Wallace McCutcheon, George Hees, and some of the others, hoping to stave off total disintegration, courageously saw Diefenbaker and suggested that he turn over the reins to Nowlan as interim Prime Minister and accept the position of Chief Justice of the Supreme Court of Canada. Diefenbaker heaped scorn on the suggestion and from then on ranked them among the growing list of his enemies.

It is instructive at this point to compare Diefenbaker's tactics and attitudes with those of Mackenzie King in the face of a similar crisis in 1944. The parallels are obvious. A crisis over defence policy, in Diefenbaker's case with the added fillip of American intervention, the resignations of key ministers, the threatened collapse of the government. King acted, while Diefenbaker waited. King moved quickly and even brutally to dismiss Ralston and replace him with McNaughton, a move which, while ineffective in a constitutional sense (since McNaughton couldn't get himself elected), was immensely profitable in buying time.

Diefenbaker, with one eye on the inimical and intimidating façade of the House, another on his fragmenting Cabinet, did nothing. He allowed Fleming and Fulton to announce they would not seek re-election; he allowed Harkness to walk out; he then allowed George Hees and Pierre Sévigny to walk out. How differently King would have reacted. King would have made sure of taking the initiative by publicly firing at least one or two of those who were leaving the sinking ship, rather than placing himself in the position of a captain being deserted by a crew who had lost confidence.

Facing the crumbling of the government, the prospect of a showdown between Canada and the United States, a deterioration of relations over nuclear arms, the only effect of which could be to damage both countries, Canadians were disturbed and uneasy. Meanwhile the Americans didn't bother to conceal their anger over the indecision and uncertainty of the Canadian government.

The resignations were a vote of non-confidence. They were intertwined with the caucus showdown in which I faced some of the mutineers and in perhaps the most difficult speech of my career fought against old friends and comrades who sincerely believed in their hearts that Diefenbaker was destroying the party and damaging the country. I fought them to a standstill because I knew what made them tick, the ingrained loyalty so strong that it would take a catastrophe to rock it. That fundamental loyalty that day saved Diefenbaker's leadership, and never a word or sign from him to me about it. It was an emotion-wracked occasion, one that will not soon be forgotten by those who took part.

But the inevitable could no longer be postponed. The Diefenbaker government subsided not with a crash but with the sound of escaping air. Defeated in the House and forced to go to the people, Diefenbaker in the 1963 election campaign showed flashes of his old form, absent in 1962. But Canadians were not buying the accusations and charges and self-justifications of a Prime Minister who couldn't control his own government. There was no way of explaining the resignations of George Hees and Pierre Sévigny, party wheel-horses both. On April 8 Lester Pearson and the Liberals were returned to office in a minority position.* Pearson took steps to have the nuclear warheads hauled into the country with fanfare, and after a few months they were quietly returned to the United States.

By this time John F. Kennedy, the young man who invested the presidency with a kind of graciousness and integrity and literacy it hadn't had since Woodrow Wilson, had been brutally and treacherously shot down on a Dallas street, a tragic crime the ramifications of which are not yet known. John Kennedy gave his life to the world and like a light in the world went out, leaving darkness behind.

The 1965 election, another stalemate,† made it clear to a large body in the Conservative Party that in spite of an incompetent and accident-prone Liberal administration we could not win without a change of leadership.

The atmosphere of division and dissension in the party proved that John Diefenbaker had lost the capacity to lead Canada and to heal the wounds within his own party. A substantial section within the party became aware of the need for a new kind of leadership which would bring unity where dissension reigned, restore confidence where all was uneasiness and distrust, and revitalize the party organization that was sinking into stagnation and desuetude because of the isolation of the leadership. This was the feeling throughout the national organization, where men like J. M. Macdonnell, Wallace McCutcheon, Egan Chambers, and

---

*(1963) Liberal 129, Progressive Conservative 95, Social Credit 24, N.D.P. 17. This was a gain of 30 seats for the Liberals, and a loss of 21 for the Conservatives.

†(1965) Liberal 131, Progressive Conservative 97, N.D.P. 21, Social Credit Rally 9, Social Credit 5, Others 2.

Dalton Camp, the National President, were in touch with a wide cross-section of the rank and file.

Even at this stage there were those who mentioned the name of Robert Stanfield, scion of a Conservative family of impeccable antecedents, who after an uphill fight had become Premier of Nova Scotia, bringing to the job a freshness of vision and administrative capacity which gained him a reputation beyond the borders of his province. Stanfield had supporters at Conservative Party headquarters, including Flora MacDonald, who had made a massive contribution to the party in five general elections. Finally, Dalton Camp, Wallace McCutcheon, and George Nowlan went to see Stanfield in Halifax to sound him out about his plans. Exhibiting the sense of honour which Canadians were later to become more familiar with, Stanfield forbade lending his name to any draft movement as long as the current leader was in office.

Others were mentioned: Duff Roblin, John Robarts, Davie Fulton. The insuperable obstacle remained: as long as there was an incumbent in the leadership, there could be no suggestion of committing anyone to the position.

Dalton Camp, with a long and honourable career in the Conservative Party, was responsible for the national campaign in 1962 and had run (unsuccessfully) in Eglinton riding in 1963 and 1965 against Mitchell Sharp. As National President he felt he must accept the responsibility of bringing home to the party and to the leader the need for change. Mr. Diefenbaker had made it plain on more than one occasion that he had no intention of giving up the leadership. Camp determined to take the case to the party itself, and in a series of speeches to party members beginning in September 1966 he issued a call for a convention where an appraisal of the leadership could be effected.

At this critical juncture the surface of Canadian political life was ruffled by the eruption, like some monster out of the deep, of what has since come to be known as the "Munsinger Affair". It would be wearisome to recapitulate all the heavy details of a sordid and insignificant little drama. Suffice it to say (that delightful phrase of Victorian writers) that seldom has so much been made by so many of so little. The elements of the story were as follows: a relationship between a Minister in the former Diefenbaker government, Sévigny, and a woman became, largely for political reasons, a full-fledged security scandal.

Mr. Justice Spence, hand-picked for the job on grounds of his particular understanding of the necessities of the situation, issued a report sharply taking to task all those involved, however remotely, in the Munsinger episode.

So much for the queasy broth of tired sex, dismal reporting, and hysterical inquiry which came out of the Munsinger case. Diefenbaker refused to put in an appearance before this judicial punchinello, on the not unreasonable assumption that eventually it would go away; and eventually it did.

Meanwhile, in November, he faced a more serious inquiry before 1,500 Conservative Party delegates gathered in annual meeting at the Château Laurier. The meeting, billed as a showdown between Diefenbaker and Dalton Camp, was in reality a showdown between Diefenbaker and the party he had led for ten years. Like Borden, like Meighen, like Bennett, he must come to an accounting of his stewardship.

Leaders are not immortal; nor should their tenure be made a condition of the party's survival. The clamour for change brought dark suggestions of some kind of hideous conspiracy across the country. Nothing of the kind. A political party asserting its right to choose its leader represents the best and finest in democracy. When such rights are questioned, democracy itself is the loser.

There were few to gainsay Diefenbaker's triumphs and achievements; but these were in the past and none could deny the sense of uneasiness about the future swelling in the ranks of the party, almost equally divided between those who wanted Diefenbaker to stay on as leader and those who knew in their bones the time was ripe for change.

Can a man lead a party divided against him? Diefenbaker had said it himself: "A leader cannot lead when he must be constantly looking behind his back." To many of us that was a convincing argument—but not in favour of his staying.

Diefenbaker made the tactical error of attacking Camp personally when it would have been politic not to do so. After all, Camp had raised an issue that concerned a great many Conservatives at every level of the party. It was his right to do so; not even Diefenbaker could deny that. The question was now one to be resolved by the general membership, not by a slanging match between Camp and Diefenbaker. The attack on Camp produced a distasteful scene in which a number of persons rose to their feet and subjected the party leader to a barrage of catcalls. It was scarcely an edifying episode.

In view of Diefenbaker's refusal to compromise on issues, the bitterness and extremism were not unexpected. I observed my commitment to nominate Dalton Camp for re-election as party president. Around this contest, between Camp and Arthur Maloney, the issue crystallized: it was felt the election would determine who controlled the party.

When Camp was re-elected the *Ottawa Journal* said in a lead editorial, written by I. Norman Smith:

> Much has been said about "loyalty" at the conference. Loyalty is a word with a ring to it, but sometimes the ring confuses thought. The real question about loyalty is "loyalty to what?" A party's loyalty should be to its traditions and its intelligent adaptations of those traditions to today's problems.

In a party sense, the crux of the dilemma was whether, in a situation of divided loyalties, the party or the leader had the greater claim. In my case, having been a Conservative since 1911, intimately associated with every leader since Borden, I knew that leaders came and leaders went, each making his contribution in accordance with his capacities and the luck of the game, yet the party was always there. The survival of our two-party system demanded the continuing presence of a second great national party to which Canadians could turn as an alternative; that party must be the Conservative Party. As a corollary, the Conservative Party must not be allowed to rend itself on the rock of one man's personality.

Sir Robert Borden never placed himself above the party;

Meighen was tempered steel and yet never believed that his conscience and mind must be the conscience and mind of the party; Bennett, no shrinking violet, recognized the party's right to decide. These were the great modern leaders of the party and in each case they acknowledged their debt to the party. Drew was no different. All of these were men of strong ego, of proud and confident cast. Should John Diefenbaker be any different?

In my nomination of Camp I said this:

> I am confident that when this meeting is over we shall leave these halls as Conservatives, as old comrades in arms, united by old memories, old associations, old loyalties. And in that union I am confident we shall be determined that this party whose achievements have made luminous vast areas in our history, must resume its historic mission of rescuing Canada from crises.

The meeting elected Dalton Camp, and Arthur Maloney went out as a good Irishman should, holding the stirrup of his chief. We could not all be of the same view or even the same mood; little in that for recrimination or dismay. Dissent is the most precious right of free men.

John Morley, who said so many things well, with his unrivalled gifts of temperateness and political maturity, said in the introduction to *On Compromise*:

> The right of thinking freely and acting independently, of using our minds without excessive awe of authority and shaping our lives without unquestioning obedience to custom, is now a finally accepted principle in some sense or other with every school of thought that has the smallest chance of commanding the future.

That, of course, was what the exercise was all about.

Rebellion is native to my character. From childhood the wrongs suffered by one people at the hands of another, no better, no more enlightened, no more decent (in the good and Irish sense of the word), burned in my soul.

The rest is anti-climax. Within a year the party convention took place in Maple Leaf Gardens, a hockey palace in Toronto (underlining the relationship between sports and politics), and the party neatly and surgically dispensed with the services of John G. Diefenbaker and replaced him with Robert Stanfield.

I had considerable admiration for Robert Stanfield. I knew him as a man of moderation and decency who would, I thought, do a great deal toward healing the wounds in the Conservative Party. One felt that under his leadership the party would go forward, leaving behind rancours and dissensions, to a new era in our political life. Stanfield's record in Nova Scotia exhibited qualities of greatness.

I have never subscribed to the myth of Diefenbaker's greatness. At one time I felt Diefenbaker would be but a footnote to history. In recent years I have changed my mind about that. We had our fallings out, it is true. But there is no hatred or destructiveness in my feeling about John Diefenbaker, any more than in my feeling about any other person who held the arduous, demanding, and self-immolating responsibilities which he held. Men have faults equal to the sum of their abilities. Men's virtues spring from the same wellsprings wherefrom they derive their failings. Some said of De Valera that he had the wellsprings of greatness. No one meeting him and looking into his eyes as I did could doubt that statement. And yet he too was not without failings. He sent Collins and the others to treat with the British and then refused to accept the agreement they signed, plunging Ireland into bloody war. And there was political ambition behind his actions.

If Diefenbaker could have achieved humility, compromise, a tendency to give a little—to show compassion for those around him—I am sure his greatness would have been written large. As it is, his legacy leaves doubt on the pages of history.

Of course, the fires of controversy burned continuously around Diefenbaker and kept on doing so after he left the leadership, simply because of his refusal to compromise on any issue. Adherence to principle is a wonderful thing; but decisions on minor and even major problems are more easily found if there is a capacity to see another point of view.

Mr. Diefenbaker's achievements and his contribution to Canada were great. Like many reformers he had a tendency to impose his views on others. South Africa's removal from the Commonwealth emphasized the principle that there could be no colour bar in that community of nations. But could that not have been emphasized without shattering the unity of an association based on fifty years of comradeship in peace and war?

The Diefenbaker government was constantly running up against the harsh facts of life. The trade structure was what it was because of the necessities of our continental position; the United States was our best customer because the Americans needed what we had to sell and because it was more economical to obtain it from us than from someone else. By the end of six years the scope of achievements — both realized and merely contemplated — had been lost in a welter of confusion, contradictions, and confrontations.

What of John Diefenbaker's personality? A man who knew exactly what he wanted. A man imbued from early youth with the purpose of being Prime Minister; intemperate, messianic; a reformer, a crusader who could not stand or countenance divisions, as for example those implied by special treatment of French Canada. Two nations, whether pronounced in English or in French, was anathema to him. There could be no compromise.

In October 1970 I gave this impression of John Diefenbaker:

Tempestuous and controversial, his barometer always at stormy, he was contemptuous of party dogma, a pragmatist who defied analysis. Yet whatever may be said against him, justly or unjustly, never could it be charged against him that he was or ever could be irrelevant in this or any society.

Almost fanatical in his determination to save us from ourselves, he refused to take into account the motivations of men and societies and was thus constantly in a position where he thought he was being betrayed by others.

Now, in 1975, looking back, I see John Diefenbaker this way:
Not every politician becomes a legend in his own lifetime.

135

Whatever else he may have failed in, John Diefenbaker can at least claim to have succeeded in that.

As a personal odyssey there is no other life story in our politics to parallel his. While earning fame and glory, he could at the same time be petty and vindictive, with a talent for spite. Forgetfulness, not to mention forgiveness, was unknown in his vocabulary.

He was never the canonized personage of charisma and TV, but a complex man with all the faults and vices seldom acknowledged in folk heroes. The press, with its propensity for labels, pictured him as "a prairie radical" or a "populist" unbeholden to Conservatism. As I saw him he was none of these things, but a pragmatic politician, an opportunist seeking and loving power, and with immense talent for gaining it.

John Diefenbaker, whatever may be said for or against him, was (and is) no run-of-the-mill politician. But he was no man of system or of ideology, only a man of instincts and insights, a man not with logic spectacles but *with an eye*.

The Press Gallery wrote of him as an "orator" —a distortion of language. For if oratory be what John Morley said it was—structure, beauty, and passion—no one could be more remote from it than John Diefenbaker. The choice and measured phrase of a Laurier or the poetry of a McGee were no more his than was the analytical power of a Meighen. But he could put on a performance.

PEARSON

Lester Pearson had something. I never knew what it was—a kind of instant receptiveness, increasingly professional over the years, backed up by real and decent concern. He always gave the impression of being genuinely interested. His fault as a politician, if it was a fault, was his ability to place himself in the other person's position: he had all the tricks of a negotiator. Finding out how one side felt, then playing it back to the other side, and vice versa. Clever diplomacy, but inappropriate in the cut and thrust of Canadian politics when most of the time nobody gives a damn how the others think.

Bow-tied, friendly Mike Pearson became Secretary of State for External Affairs in 1948, an almost immediate symbol of Canada's power-broker role in the post-war world. He built a reputation on being frank and friendly; and a system of alliances in the Press Gallery and the Public Service which nothing could shake. One of his first acts as Prime Minister was to convene a gathering of the top mandarins on Parliament Hill. Shortly after, he increased the salaries of deputy ministers.

With some difficulty he survived the Gordon Budget, when Gordon admitted he had shown his budget to private advisers. When the budget was re-written by Parliament, Pearson rejected the budget and kept Gordon, reversing the usual procedure.

He respected Parliament but was unimpressed by all its forms. He regarded Parliament as a kind of forum where you stated a case and waited for it to be accepted or rejected. It took him some time to adjust to the adversary system and to realize that Parliament was not the U.N., and that everything cannot be settled by negotiation; because, as John Kennedy pointed out in Berlin, some things are not negotiable.

Pearson feared and disliked Diefenbaker; and Diefenbaker distrusted Pearson. When they clashed there was no room for amenities or niceties, and Parliament suffered.

As a debater, Pearson was not in the same street with Diefenbaker; he had an unfortunate lisp and a high voice. His carefully prepared, set-piece speeches did not carry the conviction of Diefenbaker's theatrical performances. Pearson's speeches were always open-ended, the conclusion being left to the audience. Diefenbaker left nothing to chance. Always the courtroom attorney, he dotted every i, crossed every t, and mercilessly pinned down the guilt of those who opposed him.

Of course, Pearson was a set-up for Diefenbaker because of his conditioned instinct to bargain and back up. In the Canada Pension Plan controversies Pearson sent Tom Kent on a dramatic dash to Quebec City to find out what Lesage would settle for; and then he built these requirements into the general structure, so the country got a plan designed by Lesage.

When scandal crept into the upper reaches of his government, Pearson was feeble and indecisive; he gave a good imitation of an elderly spinster caught with a man under the bed. Instead of acting decisively to deal with the situation he issued a "Code of Ethics", a kind of Boy Scout gesture appropriate to the upper echelons of the Public Service but definitely out of place in Parliament. He suffered from an irrepressible penchant for offering the Americans unsolicited advice at times of crisis; as, for instance, suggesting a "bombing pause" when the Americans had thousands of young men being killed and wounded in Viet Nam.

Pearson was always in the position of someone pedalling a bicycle full-tilt, yelling "Look, no hands!" The problem was that now and then he forgot where the curb was. Personally, Mike Pearson was pleasant and entertaining; he failed, however, to convey any great sense of conviction.

Pearson's intolerable weakness was his incurable propensity for trying to get the best of both worlds: bringing nuclear missiles into Canada and sending them back; carrying out the recommendations of the Royal Commission on Publications, of which I was Chairman, by implementing special tax concessions for advertisers in Canadian magazines and then, in an incredible about-face, allowing the two most successful American publications to be granted the status of Canadian magazines. That was Pearson's failure, his obsession with playing both ends against the middle.

This is not the place to deal in detail with the recommendations of our report, but when the government in 1965 made a mockery of it by treating *Time* and *Reader's Digest* as though they were Canadian publications and thereby entitled to benefit from tax concessions to advertisers, it was going directly against the evidence before our commission. Mr. Henry R. Luce had appeared before us and in ringing tones stated that *Time* was not and could not be considered a Canadian magazine. Speaking in the Senate in June 1965, I put my finger on the weakness in the Pearson government with these words:

> Ottawa has been placed in the ludicrous and false position of introducing legislation of this character by pressure from Washington.

The government's decision was all the harder to bear since we had sat for over eight months, held thirty-two public hearings, travelled 7,000 miles, and sifted through 4,500 pages of evidence. In a nutshell, our conclusion was that Canadian publications were subjected to unfair, unjust, and crippling competition from so-called Canadian editions of American publications, which added up to the most vicious form of intellectual dumping. Now, after ten years it is encouraging, although almost too late for the Canadian magazine industry, to note that the government is finally prepared to act.

However, I must not appear to blame only the Pearson Liberals. When speaking to the Senate Committee on Mass Media, in February of 1970, I said:

> What I am complaining about I blame on the failure of not only one party but both, because the Conservative Government was not going

to accept my report either. . . . Somebody once said that if Moses had been a Royal Commission, the Israelites would still be in Egypt.

At the time when we held our hearings the so-called Canadian edition of *Time* magazine was edited in New York, printed in Chicago, and trucked into Canada for mailing. While revenues of Canadian magazines went down and down, those of the cuckoos in the nest went up and up. Never at any time did we suggest controlling or restricting these foreign-owned publications; we merely insisted that privileges reserved for persons buying advertising in Canadian publications should not be extended to those buying advertising in non-Canadian publications.

Perhaps I should repeat here something we said in our report which I think exemplified the role played by Canadian magazines in our community:

Canada's particular responsibilities, her Government, her constitutional structure, her ideals and aspirations, her memories and milestones, even her discords, are facts in her existence which cannot be approached understandingly or even usefully by communications media owned or controlled in another country, even though that country be friendly.

This did not in any sense mean that Canada should join the ranks of countries barring comment on their affairs by foreign journalists. What it did mean was that all or a major part of that comment should not emanate from foreign sources. Because of the Pearson government's fear of offending Washington, *Time* and *Reader's Digest* continued for more than ten years to enjoy privileges specifically assigned by Parliament to Canadian-owned publications. Meanwhile, the list of Canadian publications falling by the wayside went on apace.

On the flag issue, Mike Pearson displayed the same kind of uncertainty, beginning with a three-leaf flag and ending up with a flag bearing only a single maple leaf. He made of the flag a political issue and a personal issue, unfurling it at the Canadian Legion

Convention in Winnipeg before a hostile audience and consulting
regularly with his friends in the media while the House Committee sat.

In a Senate speech, I took strong exception to Pearson's tactics:

> What was the controversy in the House of Commons about? It was
> about whether the Flag should have on it the Union Jack or the Maple
> Leaf. So finally and sensibly, after a lot of rancorous debate the matter
> was referred to a Parliamentary Committee charged with the duty of
> seeking some fair compromise. How could the Prime Minister tell the
> nation on Sunday night that the Flag that comes from the Committee
> will be a Flag based on "this historic and proud emblem of Canada, the
> Maple Leaf"?

I spoke on the flag again on December 15, 1964, saying that
Pearson had missed a historic opportunity to put before Canadians
a flag that truly reflected the greatness of the Canadian story. For
the sake of a facile party achievement he had sacrificed an opportunity to play a role for a better and greater Canada. I added:
"Honourable Senators, you cannot take a bit of native foliage and
put it on a piece of bunting and call it a Flag."

Apparently, the Pearson government could and did. I went back
to George Brown, that "covenanting old chap" (as Macdonald
once called him), for an example of statesmanship that placed
country above party.

> Exactly a hundred years before, give a day or two one way or the
> other, George Brown, that old antagonist of John A. Macdonald,
> forgot his old enmities, forgot his grudges, and for the sake of a
> Canada whose unity was vexed at that time, for a Canada in a state of
> torment, approached his old enemy and said in effect, Canada is bigger
> than we are, we have a common love for Canada, we want Canada to
> survive and because of that, let us forget our differences and unite. . . .

Unfortunately, Mr. Pearson did not seize the opportunity offered. Lacking the stature of a Macdonald or a Brown, he was

unable to take the necessary steps to bring the Opposition into the flag project. No greater opportunity in statesmanship was missed in this century. I went on to say:

> This is the plea I make for a Flag; that it be a Flag of history, a Flag to teach history, a Flag to teach patriotism and love of country.

Posterity will decide whether the flag ushered in with closure by Mr. Pearson fulfils these conditions.

I summarized the flag issue in these terms:

> A Flag conceived in political partisanship, a Flag born in bitter political controversy, a Flag imposed on this nation by closure and a Flag which in a few days will be unfurled from the Peace Tower in utter national disunity.

A few days later the Red Ensign came down and the new flag went up.

In February 1968 Parliament faced a curious situation when a government bill imposing a three-per-cent surtax, part of the budget package, was defeated in the House during the absence of the Prime Minister (who had already announced his impending retirement) on a Caribbean holiday. In spite of demands from his own party that the government must be forced from office because of their defeat on a matter of budgetary policy, Mr. Stanfield, the new Conservative leader, chose a moderate course and decided to await Mr. Pearson's return. His moderation did not sit too well with some of his own members, including Mr. Gordon Churchill, who resigned from the Progressive Conservative caucus in February 1968. He sat as an Independent Conservative for the balance of the 27th Parliament and did not contest the 1968 election.

Stanfield met with Pearson on his return and agreed to allow the Prime Minister a twenty-four-hour breathing space to examine the situation. Pearson used the time to go on television and explain to the Canadian people that what had happened was not really a constitutional defeat but merely a fluke. He demanded a vote of confidence from the House and, by making sure all his members were present, won the vote. The Opposition's opportunity to squeeze out the government went glimmering.

Dealing with the issue in the Senate on February 20, I said:

> Her Majesty's Ministers in the other place have asked for a delay of twenty-four hours so that they can consider the matter and decide what they should do about the constitutional position created by the vote in the other place last evening. . . . I submit to Honourable Senators it would be highly improper for this House to consider a measure emanating from the Budget of which, I repeat, a vital part was rejected in the other place yesterday. . . .

I was, of course, overruled by the Liberal majority in the Senate, and business went on as usual. Stanfield, by following a course of responsibility, missed the boat politically, giving the Liberals time to rid themselves of Lester Pearson, whom Stanfield would have beaten, I am convinced, in an election. Then came the Liberal leadership convention in April that selected the brilliant and dashing Pierre Trudeau, a choice which put paid to Stanfield's hopes. And the Quebec radical reformer and activist became Prime Minister of Canada, inaugurating policies of language equality, government by task force, and "social animation".

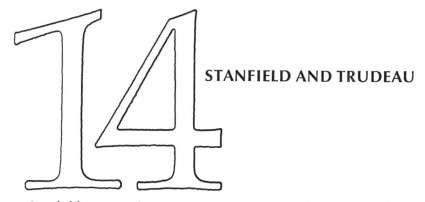

STANFIELD AND TRUDEAU

Stanfield remained unperturbed through all of this, going about his task quietly and efficiently, building up the Leader's Office, getting on with the business of organizing the party machinery. In the June 1968 election a charismatic Trudeau soundly trounced the Conservative Party.*

In the 1972 election the Stanfield team—Gerald Baldwin, Flora MacDonald, Gordon Fairweather—came within an ace of victory, holding Trudeau to a minority government.† My friend Allan MacEachen, as House Leader, spent two years pulling the government's chestnuts out of the fire with skill and dexterity; and in 1974 Trudeau was ready to go to the country again. His campaign was vigorous, aggressive, and destructive again of Stanfield's hopes of victory. On the defensive, Stanfield spent most of the campaign trying to explain what he did not intend rather than what he actually meant by his wage-price freeze policy. Once again Trudeau was Prime Minister with a solid majority.‡ At a gathering one night in Senator John Macdonald's room, Senator Macdonald mentioned that he had moved from one Ottawa hotel to another to save money. Stanfield, who was

*(1968) Liberal 155, Progressive Conservative 72, N.D.P. 22, Créditiste 14, Others 1. In 1965 the Liberals had taken 131 seats to the Conservatives' 97.

†(1972) Liberal 109, Progressive Conservative 107, N.D.P. 31, Social Credit 15, Others 2.

‡(1974) Liberal 141, Progressive Conservative 95, N.D.P. 16, Social Credit 11, Others 1.

sitting there apparently paying little attention, rose to leave. At the door he paused and turned back. "Say, John," he asked, "what are the rates at this new place?"

I suppose it was his simplicity and quiet humour one recalled most vividly when Stanfield made the announcement he was leaving the leadership.

I wrote of Stanfield in an editorial-page piece in October 1970:

> . . . a man who if or when he takes power may well be another
> Sir Robert Borden. Able, knowledgeable, with a civilized mind, a
> humanist with understanding and care for the tribulations of our day,
> Robert Stanfield is in no doubt about the Conservative philosophy,
> knows how and where and to what degree that philosophy, hostile to
> reaction, may be applied to contemporary society.

Often my heart went out to Stanfield as he laboured manfully to restore unity to a party rent by internal divisions and bitter memories. He never gave way to recrimination or name-calling. Always the same spirited, honourable gentleman who left the quiet purlieus of Nova Scotia to answer the call of his party and his country, Stanfield would have brought honour and dignity to the role of Prime Minister; unfortunately for him and for Canada this was denied him by history.

Perhaps it was the continuing rejection by Quebec which more than anything rendered his leadership an exercise in frustration. No one could say he didn't do everything possible to convince Quebecers of his sincerity. There were the immersion courses, the painful and finally successful mastery of a language not his own, the long speeches delivered before French-speaking audiences who applauded the effort and then reminded themselves of the party's neglect in not having had a French-speaking leader since Confederation. Stanfield proved the point that in spite of anything an English-language leader may do, Quebec is not about to void its ancient allegiance to the Liberal Party for any but a French Canadian, and not even that with surety.

Stanfield, of course, was not an orator. His attempts at formal speech-making conjured up all the sympathy and more rarely the support of his audiences. His speeches, long, painstaking, full of information, lacking in inspiration, left audiences unwarmed and unconvinced.

Oratory is something that comes from inside, not with texts and canned speeches. It cannot be injected or imposed. Lester Pearson was never an orator; of him it might be said that he never made a bad speech or an exciting one. Of Stanfield it could be said that at times even he appeared unconvinced by what he was saying. He came into his own with a small, intimate audience, as, for example, the annual Press Gallery dinner. It would certainly come as a surprise to many who heard Stanfield speak over the years that before this most discriminating of audiences his reputation as a wit and a humorist is forever secure.

But the man himself, that is more important. Here is what I said about him in 1974 to a national gathering in Toronto of the Progressive Conservative Youth Association—and in the year and more since then my respect and personal regard for him are greater still:

> David Lloyd George once said of Dr. Clifford, the great Baptist divine, that there was no man in England upon whose conscience he would sooner ring a coin.
>
> That, in Canada, can be said of Robert Stanfield.
>
> There are public men who, because of certain qualities, sometimes called charisma, attain to temporary popularity. But there are other men who, through deeper things of conduct and character, light enduring beacon fires of public trust and affection. One of these, unquestionably, is Robert Stanfield. When, regretfully for us, he puts off his armour, I hope that memory will hold the door. The memory of a leader who loved truth more than he loved applause. Who hated cant and humbug. Who made the quality of human life the true measure of our growth as a nation. Who could discipline compassion with common sense. Who could fight the encroachments of a leviathan state upon the liberty of the individual, yet understand where the sovereign domain of the individual begins and ends. Who, above all, left his party a priceless heritage of integrity.

Pierre Elliott Trudeau, first elected to Parliament in 1965, became Prime Minister after serving a term as Minister of Justice and distinguishing himself before the television cameras at a federal-provincial conference. He was truly a child of the media. In early middle age (though he himself wasn't too sure how old he was), he was a representative of the New Wave in politics, a sort of bilingual John Kennedy, mixed with D'Artagnan of the Three Musketeers.

He even had his Aramis and Porthos in the personalities of Gérard Pelletier, a former editor of *La Presse*, and Jean Marchand, fiery and tempestuous, a major figure in the strongly organized Quebec labour movement. When Trudeau became Prime Minister after a convention at which he knocked out some long-time and leading Liberals like R. H. Winters, Allan MacEachen, and Paul Martin (accused in the press of tinting his temples), Pelletier and Marchand were given Cabinet jobs.

Trudeau made it plain his intention was to reassert a strong federal presence in Canada and a strong French-Canadian presence in the federal government. In this his thinking was not too far removed from Louis St. Laurent's.

An intellectual, Trudeau was that rare combination, an academic who was also a man of action. Not content with writing about the bloody asbestos strike in 1949, he took an active part. As for separatists, "indépendantistes", radicals, apostles of the Quebec Revolution, he knew personally all the movers and shakers in the province, having worked with many of them on *Cité Libre*, a radical journal founded by Trudeau and Pelletier in order to get at Duplessis. In its pages he had published his merciless attack on Lester Pearson's nuclear policy in 1963.

I summed up my views on Trudeau in an editorial-page piece in October 1970:

> ... attractive, intelligent, exciting, the antithesis of the stodgy mysticism of a Mackenzie King or the amiable ways of a Lester Pearson who (as Harold Macmillan said of Neville Chamberlain) was "a good man in the worst sense of the word". But Trudeau's "style", his Rudolph Valentino pull for females who want to be "liberated", hardly suffices for high unemployment or the fact that one-third of Canada's population is under the poverty line. ...

The most critical test of Trudeau's policies came that same month, when Canada was caught in the grip of a crisis unparalleled since the 1837 Rebellion.

Canadians, having heard and read about guerrilla revolutionary movements, the offspring of radical disaffection in other countries, discovered that we in this nation were harbouring one of the most violent and virulent of these movements in our midst. First a British diplomat, James Cross, was kidnapped. Then Pierre Laporte, a minister in the Quebec government, a former member of the Parliamentary Press Gallery, was kidnapped too; he was later found brutally murdered. For these crimes, committed by two apparently separate cells of the Quebec Liberation Front (F.L.Q.), a Marxist-style underground group of young fanatics, there had been plenty of advance warning.

A few years earlier, the province had experienced an outbreak of gun thefts in armouries and hardware stores by young fanatics under the leadership of a Belgian called Schoeters, trained in Cuba, and a former Algerian freedom-fighter called François Schrim. Both these men were caught and imprisoned; but this was only the beginning.

These unsavoury episodes were followed by bombings of federal buildings, the blowing up of federal symbols such as mailboxes, and carefully orchestrated demonstrations on issues of race and language, all in the familiar Marxist pattern of setting class against class and race against race. The result was a state of tension unknown to Quebec since 1837. Paradoxically the situation contributed to Trudeau's winning the 1968 election when, at a St. Jean Baptiste parade in Montreal on the eve of the election, he revealed to television viewers his cool courage and contempt for rioting demonstrators.

The kidnappings and the death of Laporte were followed by demands for the release of so-called "political prisoners", jailed because of participation in bomb-throwings and robberies in which at least two deaths had occurred; the payment of a vast sum of money to the kidnappers by the Quebec government; and transportation to Cuba or Algeria, way stations of Marxist revolutionary activity.

The City of Montreal, where the kidnappings had taken place, and the Government of Quebec, appealed to Ottawa, alleging a state of affairs inimical to the preservation of law and order and the protection of citizens. The Prime Minister sought and gained Parliament's approval for emergency measures based on the War Measures Act, the only legislative enactment which permitted him to take strong and immediate action. Troops were sent into Quebec to assist the civil authorities in maintaining law and order; numbers of persons of separatist and radical backgrounds were rounded up and questioned. The Prime Minister ordered the immediate cutting off of F.L.Q. propaganda from the province's air waves. As French-speaking paratroopers from Edmonton were clambering out of helicopters in the streets of Montreal, troops in Ottawa took up guard duty on the premises of government ministers and leading parliamentarians.

One of the strange incidents was the offer conveyed through Lucien Saulnier, head of the Executive Council of Montreal, by separatist leader René Lévesque and the heads of three major unions—Louis Laberge of the Quebec Federation of Labour, Marcel Pépin of the Quebec Syndicates, and Yvon Charbonneau of the Teachers' Union—to take positions in the Bourassa government, apparently to mediate the crisis. Bourassa did not see fit to accept.

I knew the pressure Trudeau must be enduring as the ill-omened F.L.Q. adventure threatened to destroy everything he had been working for, particularly the confidence of English-speaking Canadians that Quebec could be satisfied with reasonable and progressive gains within the existing structure.

I admired Trudeau's conduct. The situation, which had been deteriorating over a period of years with the assistance of foreign agitators allowed into Quebec, needed badly to be pulled together. Trudeau acted with firmness and promptness. The agony on his face at the news of Pierre Laporte's death by strangulation cannot soon be forgotten.

Recourse by the government to the War Measures Act brought out, like genii from a bottle, a horde of critical commentators big with knowledge gained by abstract contemplation of events from the security of an Ontario or British Columbia campus. From such

149

vantage points they gained immediate insights into problems they had seldom previously heard of; became instant experts in the complexities of Quebec politics, knotted and ravelled in a thousand cords from Confederation until the present.

Undeterred by Gordian knots, in they rushed, brimming with exhortations, admonitions, prescriptions, into the pages of the political science journals; crusaders for civil rights, they forgot the fundamental truth that freedom cannot be erected on the bones of the innocent.

There were greater issues at stake than political careers and the survival of governments. In the Senate I made the statement, "You cannot condone murder." I am quite certain that only the immediate and heavy pressure put on by the Canadian government resulted in securing the release of the British consular official James Cross unharmed. A group of kidnappers flew away to Cuba, their dreams of political power adrift in the half-light of the Marxist other world.

On October 27, 1970, in the Senate, I made my basic position very clear:

> I now come to the tragic events that have oppressed and distressed this country during the past two or three weeks. Let me say at the beginning without reservation and without equivocation that I support absolutely and wholeheartedly the resort to the War Measures Act in the circumstances that existed.

Of the War Measures Act I said, "The Government had no other weapon to fight the tyranny and horror that came to us." I firmly believe that to be so. Every aspect of the criminal acts showed they had been carefully planned over a period of time. Young people had been recruited from various independence and radical groups to become kidnappers and murderers in the name of a cause of whose true nature they were not even aware. Some of their leaders had spent weeks and months in Cuba learning the intricacies of automatic carbines and the use of cheap Chinese alarm clocks in the manufacture of home-made bombs.

A number of questions remained to be answered. How could

armed revolutionary organizations spring up undetected on the soil of Quebec? Where were the security measures? What were the relations between the various groups which for several years had kept the province in turmoil? How were they being financed?

Curiously, these were among the matters raised before a parliamentary committee by Lucien Saulnier a few months before the outbreak of guerrilla violence. No answers were ever provided.

I warned Prime Minister Trudeau about what might be an Achilles heel in his general posture:

> Having said what I have, having given wholehearted support to the Government action in the circumstances that existed I feel it my duty to add this. There is a dark and misty area in the situation over the past three weeks that needs answers by the Government with clarity and candour.

What evidence did the government possess indicating a possibility of civil insurrection? None was ever forthcoming, although the Prime Minister on more than one occasion spoke of "further revelations". They never came. Canadians are no wiser today as to the full ramifications of these dreadful episodes than they were then.

In the Senate, I said:

> He [the Prime Minister] is not sitting in the Kremlin; he is sitting in the Parliament of Canada and he is accountable. If you do not have accountability and if you can invoke an act such as the War Measures Act which is one of the most extraordinary actions undertaken in the history of this country outside of wartime, then surely the duty devolves upon you to tell the people why you had to do it.

What unrevealed or unspoken motivations impelled the Prime Minister to measures that, thank God, few Canadian prime ministers have had to justify have never been made public. These things are not unique, but they are extraordinary. One recalls vividly Louis St. Laurent as Minister of Justice acting under the

151

Emergency Powers Act to hold those accused in the Gouzenko affair without charges and without warrants incommunicado for ten days. Extraordinary situations demand extraordinary measures. When we in the democracies lose the capacity to deal with extraordinary and emergent crises, then we shall not long survive our own vulnerability.

I was particularly affected by these events. I have never subscribed to the theory that Quebec citizenship must be reserved for French Canadians alone: I was and am a Quebecer; I thought I knew and understood French Canadians.

I have always been concerned about the question of Quebec's relations with the rest of Canada. It is a question which has interested me as a Canadian and a Quebecer. In the Senate in December 1963 I spoke on the bill to set up a National Centennial Commission:

> I am a child of Quebec. I was born within a few miles of the spot where Jacques Cartier planted his cross in Gaspé. . . .
>
> I think it is true there was a Canada, certainly the name Canada, long before the Act of 1867. But we are not proposing in 1967 to celebrate a centennial or tercentenary of Canada. What we are proposing to celebrate is an Act of the Imperial Parliament passed in 1867; and surely no one will deny that act did in fact, set up a state, a political entity on this continent.

An Irish upbringing and a Quebec boyhood combined to produce deep sympathy for the aspirations of French Canadians and high admiration for the moderation and skill with which over the years they consistently pursued their goals within the framework of the constitutional structure. This vicious and violent outburst accompanied by imported revolutionary claptrap did not reflect French Canadians as I knew them.

I was annoyed with those who said that this sort of thing happened only in Quebec. "As one who boasts that two generations of those who began my days sleep in the soil of Quebec I reject and resent that." I was reminded of Edmund Burke's statement, "You cannot, sir, indict a people."

PERSONAL AND PROFESSIONAL LIFE

I must be mindful in writing my "life" to speak of those who meant the most to me. Fortune being my friend, some politicians were among my most intimate friends. But I want now to say some personal words about my wife and family, of my companions over fifty-five years at the *Journal*, and of my friends who were not blessed, or cursed, with the surge of politics. A look at my life without a glimpse of what Duncan Campbell Scott called the "circle of affection" would miss my life.

Even so, it is hard to write of one's family — we were all close and loving, yet hesitant to say so. I take the easy way out by repeating some lines I. Norman Smith wrote about our home in his sensitive book *The Journal Men* on the lives and times of P. D. Ross, E. Norman Smith, and myself:

The year 1913 brought a great event [to Grattan]—his marriage on July 1 to Mary Honoria McKenna, daughter of Arthur McKenna and Catharine Murphy, of Antigonish, Nova Scotia. His bride had been a gold medallist at St. Bernard's College, St. Francis Xavier University. After teaching briefly in the United States she had come to Ottawa to work in the Auditor General's Department. Even when I came to know them 20 or more years later they seemed a young couple, the house alive with children and their friends, with fun and laughter and dogs and argument. There was always good controversy on books and politics and sport and—yes—on art and religion and humanity. In latter years Mrs. O'Leary suffered greatly from arthritis, but rarely did her smile and manner lack its old compassion and humor.

They had five children and, you might say, the seven grew up together. I recall few if any families of those 20's and 30's where the relationship between parents and children was so natural and as vigorous in its cohesive affection, though a family of seven very separate individuals. Dillon and Brian became good newspapermen in their own right, though Brian died in 1971. Dillon writes thoughtful editorials, book reviews and a cheery column on wine for the *Journal*. Owen, a Pilot Officer in the R.A.F., was killed in World War II. Maurice moved from the bottom to vice president, technology, in the Aluminum Company of Canada. The one daughter, Moira, married Frank McGee. The latter as newspaperman, public relations executive, member of parliament and grand-nephew of Thomas D'Arcy McGee, needed no spur to his Conservative persuasion. But he got it from his wife, in O'Leary-like daily dialectics, lively and loud and with the clout of a handsome woman.*

Norman sees us well, I think, though generously. But I add with grateful love that dear Mollie was the heart's desire of us all, the master of the house, you might say.

There has been another family in my life—the *Journal* family. When I retired as President of the *Journal* in 1966, I had spent fifty-six years if not at the same desk at least on the same paper. I recall each one of those years with affection and nostalgia. I have mentioned the *Journal* and several of its people in earlier pages but now I want to spend a little time with them personally.

P. D. Ross was a fine gentleman, a great sportsman, a fighting newspaperman, and a crusader for Canada. Sham he hated, but, as I have remarked before, he had understanding and compassion, the gift of forgiveness. His concern for the quality of justice left him with a haunting fear lest by tongue or pen he had in haste inflicted hurt or wrong. That was the kind of man he was. Ross wasn't as good a writer as John Dafoe, but was a fairer and broader man, with warmer literary and artistic senses. I was not as high on Dafoe as some of his followers; he had the weaknesses as well as the strengths of being a thundering Westerner. But take Ross's editorial on the death of Sir John A. Macdonald, or his courageous

---

*From *The Journal Men* by I. Norman Smith.

attack on the injustice to Riel; they are magnificent, and they could come only from a large heart and a ranging mind.

His associates in the *Journal* had great pride in his stature. He was never a slavish follower of party shibboleths or of party leaders. Stout in his independence, he maintained his own beliefs against all temptations of friendship or the influence of his private relations with public men. He did not change his views of a question because his party took a particular course and its fortunes were at stake. Nor would he descend to abuse. He said to his editors, "Condemn a man's politics as much as you like but leave his personality alone." It was perhaps a tribute to his precept and example that in later years, when his pen was largely put aside, he never disagreed with his associates' policies or with their method of expressing them.

In religion P. D. Ross had the gift of reverence. He was never the materialist. His adult life spanned all the swift drama of change in three-quarters of a century, but on the fiftieth anniversary of the *Journal*, giving his impressions of it all, he closed on this note:

> There is the same old need, the same overwhelming need, of love and faith, of honesty and generosity, of unselfishness and neighborliness, of clean conduct and fair play. And the truth remains as much as it did fifty years ago that these last mentioned things are more important to humanity than all the achievements of art and science and mechanical invention from the beginning of the world, or all there can be to the end of it.

What an extraordinary man, really! I remember well the affection and respect with which E. Norman Smith and I and several of our associates talked of the shape our editorial should take when we knew P.D.'s death was at hand, at ninety-one. And, forgive the pride, I remember, too, my emotion when Mr. Smith, on reading my draft of our closing lines, came quietly into my office with a bit of a catch in his voice and said simply, "Thank you, Grattan, don't touch it; thank you." He walked back to his room and gently closed the door. We all felt that way. The editorial ended with these words:

> P. D. Ross never moved in the closed circle of material satisfaction and untroubled self-approval; he was incapable of gross self-seeking or of anything that brought hurt to sensitiveness, to spiritual faith, to naked lonely thought. Yet his goodness was never unctuous, never paraded, but goodness for its own sake—goodness as a shining adventure, never without hope. . . . To the wise mind, to the valiant heart, to the loyal, constant friend, to the great soul who loved all things manly and clean; to P. D. Ross, Hail and Farewell!

E. Norman Smith brought the *Ottawa Free Press* into amalgamation with the *Journal* in 1917 and with P. D. Ross was a major architect of the paper's fortunes for over forty years. Fondly do I remember our abiding friendship and close association in our life's work and our ideals from 1917 until his death in 1957. As Editor-in-Chief he had one ruling passion: responsibility. With the *Manchester Guardian's* great C. P. Scott he believed profoundly that while comment must be free, facts were sacred. Sensationalism, the newspaper stunt, anything that violated the canons of good taste, these were abominations.

Yet with these rigid standards he was a wise and understanding colleague, with an extraordinary degree of open-mindedness and intellectual generosity, a sort of liberalism in personal relations. He never tried, as many editors and publishers find it impossible not to try, to use others as instruments for the expression of his own ideas. E. Norman Smith's own writing was never "fine" writing, not as good as P. D. Ross's. He would say no more than would convey the thought, and let the argument stand without trying to decorate it with epigram or wit or to score it with emotional undertones. This passion for the spare and simple sentence made him superb as an editor. After all, what makes a great journalist? It is not just writing. You could be the greatest writer in the world and be a hell of a poor journalist. E. Norman Smith was a great craftsman in all that went into assembling a good newspaper. He was publisher as well as editor, knew about presses and types and the problems of mechanical departments, as he knew about advertising and circulation and the general business of the company.

Though he held the editorial page to be the heart of the paper his true passion was for the news. He was to the end a working journalist, never happier than when out in the newsroom taking a hand in the presentation of some big word from the wires. Here, with "ink on his fingers", he was at home, using all the professional skills and know-how that could belong only to one whose career as a journalist took him back to the Parnell Commission in 1889, which he witnessed while on the staff of the British Press Association. He could recall vividly Parnell before the Commission and the cross-examination of Pigott by Sir Charles Russell.

P. D. Ross never looked at the editorials after E. Norman Smith was there. We were all three good friends but Mr. Smith was the editor, absolutely. There just weren't any office politics—and no friction. The political outlook of E. Norman Smith was not easy to define. It was fundamentally liberal, tempered by a touch of Victorianism, or perhaps traditionalism, and he learned to look for the liberal spirit in a wider field than the confines of any party. He took no part in politics himself; so long as his newspaper adhered to a party's principles without slavishly following a party line, he was content. He held stoutly that a newspaper's prime function was to publish the news as it comes, no matter what party it helps or injures, and that truth works for decency and moderation in human affairs. It was this belief, a passion for honest and uncoloured news, which brought him to the forefront—indeed made him one of the chief architects in providing Canada with an independent national news service: the Canadian Press.

E. Norman Smith's standards were exacting, a reflection of his own integrity and of his constant realization that the *Journal* was far more than a business—that it was a public trust.

I. Norman Smith, who followed me as Editor and President, combined two rare talents — a good literary mind and a good business mind. Very few journalists that I have known had so orderly and logical a mind. For years he was a keen aid to P. D. Ross, to his father, and to me, in maintaining the *Journal's* reputation, but as we three successively got pretty old he carried the pressure, adding his own qualities to the paper's name.

Norman began as office boy and junior clerk in business. After a year he came upstairs to news and was greeted by some with understandable suspicion. He started with the problem of being who he was! I must confess he was a bit bumptious in his early days, but he got over that fast! I remember counselling my colleagues: "Give the boy a chance, let him show whether or not he's got it." Norman didn't let me down.

After a couple of years with us Norman itched to get out on his own and got a job with the Canadian Press. After serving as reporter and desk editor in various Canadian cities they sent him to New York and then to London as news editor. It was there he picked up his lasting interest in foreign affairs—in 1955 he won the National Newspaper Award for foreign correspondence.

When, after seven or eight years with C P, Norman returned to the *Journal,* I found his ability to be out of the ordinary; he was an unusual thinker and writer—of the type contemporaries too often like to disparage. His one fault was over-writing. I remember his father coming to me and saying: "Grattan, can't we do something to get Norman to shorten his paragraphs? He writes too long." Having my own problems in that regard I suggested that perhaps as his father he had more chance of success in urging that. But the father was right.

Besides his work, Norman loved music, sports, books, and poetry—and the outdoors in winter and summer. His writing has an imaginative quality, something rare in Canada today. For example, he wrote these lines about me in his book *The Journal Men:* "... Too old to be a pessimist, alight with interest and caring for 'all in this house'—his house being all Canada, and beyond." I've often said his piece from the Press Gallery on the Pipeline Debate was one of the strongest and sharpest on that outrage. When they tore up the rules of the House he felt they were tearing up his citizenship papers. A few months ago I got a warm-hearted letter from George Ferguson—former editor of the *Winnipeg Free Press* and the *Montreal Star* — regretting what he had heard about my health. After nostalgic yet spirited talk of old, unhappy, far-off things, he closed off: "I hope you see something of Norman Smith; one of the few men I know who, like you, loves the beauty of words."

Norman became highly regarded by his *Journal* colleagues, and the respect other newspapermen bore him was shown when they elected him President of the Canadian Press, and, before that, Chairman of the Canadian Section of the Commonwealth Press Union.

But I think of Norman mainly as a dear friend, though perhaps too generous to me. At a *Journal* party a while back I put it this way:

> Everything Norman says in that book of his about P. D. Ross and his father I subscribe to warmly. But I am leery about what he says about O'Leary. However, when I reach the pearly gates which may be soon, and Peter asks me what I have to declare, I will say to him, "For Pete's sake haven't you read Norman Smith's book?" That should let me in.

But our *Journal* team was more than its chiefs or the sum of its chiefs. Heaven knows what kind of a paper we would have put out without the lovable Tommy Lowrey, surely as good a managing editor (for thirty-three years!) as any paper ever had; certainly none could have been more loyal or more respected in his community. Then there was Vernon Kipp, whose editorials were of a pure English increasingly rare in journalism, a widely read man whose shyness discouraged acclaim. May the unnamed forgive me for naming a few more: those three fine Scots, Jim McCook, Tom Johnstone, and George Paterson; the sports men Baz O'Meara, Walter Gilhooly, Bill Westwick (I have to say Bill was the best!), and Eddie MacCabe; and those two younger and able *Journal* men carrying today's battles in the heat of the sun — Lou Lalonde, the President, and John Grace, the Editorial-Page Editor. In a way I don't envy those two the restlessness and complexity of today's challenges, yet I would like to be still in there with them, as I know P. D. Ross and the two Norman Smiths would. The *Journal* was a good place to work, and we worked together as friends — not only those I have named but dozens of others, including those in the mechanical, advertising, circulation, and business departments. A man is lucky to be able to look back at the shop and to think of his old colleagues with a smile in his heart and a moistness in his eye.

Outside the shop, too, I was blessed with friends—friends large and small in stature, status, education, health, wealth, and humour. We shared ideas; we shared sports or reading or good talk, politics or poker, banter or dispute, the Ottawa Valley or all Canada and beyond. To name even fifty would leave out more than fifty. I will say only that all of them enriched my life and I thank them all and thank God for all of them.

I have touched earlier on journalism in several places but there are perhaps other press and information matters to mention—for after all, journalism was my trade. Sometimes in mischievous moments I see it this way: I know of no life that must be so delicious as that of a writer for newspapers — to thunder forth accusations against men in power; to show up the worst side of everything that is produced; to pick holes in every coat; to be indignant, sarcastic, moral, or supercilious; to damn with faint praise; to crush with open calumny!

But of course it has its other sides, such as responsibility! And, as P. D. Ross used to say, the first duty of a newspaper (or a magazine, I suppose) is to survive. This means a knowing acquaintance with all phases of newspaper work — which I did not have. But I was lucky, for Mr. Ross and E. Norman Smith had a tough, long, and broad experience in the whole challenge of publishing; and I. Norman Smith, though his main interest was news and editorial, had also a good general training in publishing.

When Mr. Ross died in 1949, I was named Vice-President to E. Norman Smith. I had been Associate Editor since 1932. When Mr. Smith died in 1957, I. Norman Smith urged me to take the presidency, though I had few shares in the company, and with him as Vice-President we set to work as "top brass"—an unlikely and unimagined role for me! It was a great honour and great fun. To tell the truth I found the responsibilities of "control" of the paper fascinating. It was specially interesting to find myself on the other side of the table in talking with "labour"—and cheering to find we could get along as friends as we always had in the *Journal*. Frankly, I think some of my colleagues were surprised to find I could add and subtract, as well as write editorials! In any event, all gave me the best team comradeship a man could have, and we were graced with a sense of humour in rough and smooth.

It is true that during my presidency—in 1959—we joined the FP group of newspapers, but this was a step that P. D. Ross and E. Norman Smith had long years earlier said would become inevitable. A paper on small resources and bank loans could not, in the new pressures of modern publishing, stand alone against large newspaper chains—at any rate not in the same city! In complete agreement, I.N.S. and I decided that in the light of the precarious nature of the *Journal's* ownership the most certain and perhaps the only way to assure its continuity was to join a reputable man and paper like Victor Sifton and the *Winnipeg Free Press*. The story of our joining the FP is well and honestly told in Norman's book *The Journal Men*, and I agree with every word and sentiment in it. It was a sad time for both of us, of course, but even on looking back I am convinced we did what had to be done. I remember saying to some economic club or other, in 1956, that I had been trying for the last year or two to get out a newspaper by the grace of God and the bank. That was true.

The question of small newspapers versus newspaper chains is much misunderstood. When I entered journalism in Saint John, New Brunswick, there were five daily newspapers propounding a variety of political opinions. Recently, the last independent daily in New Brunswick, the *Fredericton Gleaner*, went under chain ownership, a situation which does not favour personal journalism. A great deal depends on the people who control the chains.

But when I was asked in the Senate whether I thought the trend to chains would continue, I replied that it would altogether depend on the financial and economic conditions. There was not a desire by the proprietors of independent papers to become group papers: there was an economic compulsion, a question of survival. "I would have liked," I told the Senate, "and I am sure my friend

Norman Smith would have liked, to go on running the *Journal* as we were running it. We owned it, we were happy with it, and we thought we knew what a newspaper should be."

Some people, astonishingly, think the question of whether a paper is alone or one of a group somehow relates to "freedom of the press". Few terms in public debate are less understood.

Down the years I have spoken and written about what is loosely called "freedom of the press"; sometimes, to the scandal of my colleagues in the press, on the side of responsibility rather than licence. Freedom of the press is limited to the right to print truth; the truth is its own justification. It does not go beyond that. I have never subscribed to the view that because someone writes for publication or goes about with a press card stuck in his hat that person should have rights denied the ordinary individual. I know that is a general assumption; and it is wrong. All men are equal under the law; without that, the system of law can't be maintained. Whatever privileges or guarantees are implicit in the theory of freedom of the press are granted not to the individual but to the printed word. The written word has certain privileges clearly defined in our courts.

I dealt with the question in the Senate in March 1969:

> The ownership of the press, of the communications media in Canada, is a subject which should engage our serious attention. There are three areas in the structure of the nation which the people of that nation should control. The first is banking, the second is transportation, the third but not least important is communications.

As Chairman of the Royal Commission on Publications, it was my duty to help to draw up recommendations dealing with Canadian periodical publishing. I said then:

> Personally, I still feel that I would not give a licence, charter or any authority whatsoever to any person to publish a Canadian publication or newspaper or magazine or any other periodical in Canada, unless they held a Canadian passport.

In my career as a newspaperman, I always understood that I

was not the beneficiary of special privilege. When I hear people rise and quote that poetic declamation of Milton's, "Give me the liberty to know, to utter, and to argue freely according to conscience, above all liberties", I am sometimes rather amused. The right to utter treason? To utter language damaging to security? The right to incite a riot? The right, as Mr. Justice Holmes put it, to rise in a crowded theatre and shout, "Fire!"?

From time to time the idea of a Press Council comes up, a body with the function of riding herd on the press. Personally, I would be against the government's being in a position to impose guidelines on the media, particularly on the press. A voluntary Press Council, representing the press agencies themselves, would be a lesser evil; but it could also conceivably act as a brake on clear dissemination of news. My own view is that what with parliamentary committees, advertisers, subscribers, university task forces, and others, there are enough people second-guessing the press as it is.

I spoke on this subject in the Senate in January 1971:

I am suspicious of the state. I do not want the state to have anything much to do with the press. . . . I do not see how a Press Council could bring any good to the press. It has certainly brought no good to the press of England. England has had a Press Council for eight or ten years and it has been headed by very able people, the last of whom was Lord Devlin, one of the most distinguished jurists.

What has happened to the press of England under a Press Council? I lived through the golden years of British journalism. The years of C. P. Scott of the Manchester Guardian and Henry Nevinson, a knight errant of journalism. The years of C. E. Montague and Justin McCarthy, the great historian who was writing the leaders for the News and Leader. . . .

I went on to mention A. G. Gardiner and Wickham Steed and J. A. Spender. I could have mentioned Chesterton and Wells and even Edgar Wallace, who did his stint as a journalist. It is not the same now. Even *The Times* under Lord Thomson is not what it was.

There are outstanding journalists in the United States. "Scotty"

Reston, now that Lippmann and Duranty are gone, is probably the most respected. There is a tremendous amount of "in-depth" reporting coming out of the United States. Watergate was an example. How much will live? Expanding a good news story to fill a book doesn't necessarily add up to monumental literature.

In England there is no one to succeed the editorial giants of years ago, just as in Canada one looks in vain for successors to Sir John Willison, P. D. Ross, Henri Bourassa, Nicholas Flood Davin, John W. Dafoe. We have destroyed our party press. Strong editorial comment is inseparable from party affiliation. Unless it is a party press, it will not be a great press. Without a party press in England there never would have been freedom of the press as we know it. Men have got to believe in something beyond the vehicle by which they earn their daily bread.

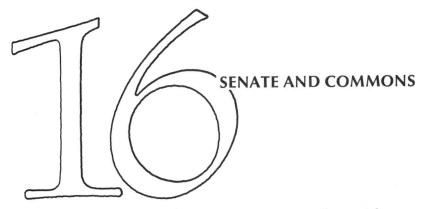

SENATE AND COMMONS

I retired as president of the *Journal* at seventy-eight to make way for younger blood (though Norman Smith pleaded with me to stay on and fitted out for me just down the hall my favourite old *Journal* room with all my stuff and books and files and battered typewriter). I say I was seventy-eight although at the time I was convinced I was seventy-six years old. It was only a couple of years ago that my half-brother in Gaspé turned up some old records showing that I was actually two years older than I thought. Now, two years may not seem much to some people; but when it carries you up nearly to the eighty mark, it can have an effect. It makes you think of your future.

I was now free to devote myself to my duties as a Senator, to grapple with some of the great national problems, and to try to win back at poker some of the money I had lost over the years.

I had not forgotten what I wrote twenty-five years earlier and what George Ferguson of the *Montreal Star,* with that acumen which made him a great newspaperman, dug up when I was appointed to the Senate:

A senatorship isn't a job. It's a title. Also it's a blessing, a stroke of good fate; something like drawing to a royal straight flush.

When I wrote that years ago I wasn't a Senator; and I had no anticipation of being appointed. Now after all these years I had to go to work to prove myself wrong.

When I accepted an appointment to the Senate it was not to participate in the destruction of that institution. The Senate is a living part of Parliament with equal rights to those of the House of Commons. On more than one occasion I have taken a stand in defence of the Senate's privileges.

In March 1964 I raised objections when, after dallying with supplementary estimates for two weeks, the House compelled the Senate to sit on Good Friday in order to await the arrival of the estimates. I regarded this as cavalier treatment of an institution which is in every way part of Parliament.

One of the items in the estimates concerned unemployment insurance funds and I was strongly criticized on the grounds that my action held up payment of benefits to the unemployed. This was, of course, a spurious accusation. If the government thought no more of the unemployed than to delay securing an allocation of funds until a few days before they ran out, I could hardly be blamed for their neglect. I said:

> This business of calling us back like messenger boys is not only an affront to the Senate but because the Senate is an integral part of Parliament I think it is an insult to Parliament itself.

Some people were scandalized at my attitude. I was called "The Last Angry Man of the Senate" and things of that sort. I managed to survive. The unemployed who could not collect their cheques were victims of rank government incompetence, not my intransigence. I was described as "petulant, peevish, rash, and irresponsible". The *Globe and Mail* in a rush of self-righteous indignation suggested my seat be abolished.

What had happened? The Senate was told only at five in the afternoon that a bill was coming over from the other House. The bill arrived at half past five. The Senate was asked to put through something like $135 million in half an hour, otherwise the Governor General might miss his dinner. Is this democracy?

It was not, in my estimation, any way to run a country. I said so, in moderate and reasoned terms, and for that was belaboured on all sides. I didn't mind that. What I minded was the slight to Parliament.

On April 6, I said:

I do not rise to apologize for, to recede or to retreat one inch from the course which I took last Friday with respect to this bill. To quote from one who was long my hero in public life, the course that I took on Friday last stands unrevised and unrepented.

I am sure that Arthur Meighen, could he have known, would have been proud of my stand.

I warned that if the Senate forgot its rights and responsibilities no one else would remember them.

If we permit others to trample on those rights or to despise them we condemn this House to a place of inconsequence, a place for only ceremony and ritual, a place with no meaningful legislative existence.

The Senate has amply repaid the confidence of its founders. Its membership, generally composed of men and women of experience in public affairs, fleshed out by those who have sat for many years in the Commons, quite often on the Treasury benches, represents a cross-section of achievement in every walk of life. What it would cost the nation to have at its beck and call the advisory services of some of the people sitting in the Senate at a very nominal remuneration staggers the imagination.

Some of those most vociferous in talking Senate "reform" are really more concerned with abolishing the Senate, removing it as an evil or an inconvenience standing in the way of more general reforms, or even of radical reconstruction which they would like to impose on the social structure. The Senate, acting with courage and conviction, stands as a guardian of the gateway of freedom, and I hope always will.

In February 1969 speaking in defence of the Senate, I said:

I am under no illusions as to what some of the public think. What they are hoping for is not reform of the Senate but castration of the Senate.

Parliament's primary function is to check the acts and proposals of the Executive. In casting about for a more important role for the Senate, I have suggested an examination of the hundreds of

Orders-in-Council issuing from government departments. Seventy-five per cent of all administrative acts undertaken by government are taken by Order-in-Council. One of the Senate's constitutional duties is to protect minorities, and in this case the public is a minority at the mercy of decisions taken by powerful bureaucrats, boards, commissions, agencies, and departments. The Senate could perform a useful service by scrutinizing orders and directives to determine whether they infringe the liberties of subjects in this country.

We are told that the public is critical of Parliament. Thank God for that. The public has always been critical of Parliament. That has been its salvation. I think it was Charles Dickens who said Parliament was an insane asylum run by the inmates.

The most vital function the Senate can perform is to stand between the people — the taxpayers — and the encroachments of the all-powerful bureaucracy.

Senate reform? Of course; but how do you reform the Senate? By naming people whose wit and wisdom at the service of Canadians will provide a safety valve, a machinery of second-guessing, to some extent at least removed from the pressures of pure partisanship. In recent years the Senate has twice interposed between the government and the House the device of "sober second thought" as Macdonald called it.

The first occasion was when the Senate turned back legislation proposed under the Diefenbaker government relating to anti-dumping provisions and giving the minister discretion under the law to decide the conditions of liability in each case. The Senate rightly concluded this was giving too much power to the minister and turned the bill back to the House.

The other case was, of course, the celebrated Coyne episode when the Governor of the Bank of Canada, refused a hearing by the Commons, was granted one by a highly partisan and Liberal-dominated Senate. Frankly, I don't think Coyne deserved a hearing any more than any other public servant who disagrees with government policy; resignation under the circumstances is one of the conditions of employment. Coyne, like many other Liberal appointees at the time with the whole weight of the Liberal hierarchy behind them, felt a duty to defy an upstart Conservative administration in power for the first time in twenty-two years.

The Senate, of course, should not be a partisan instrument; to reduce it to that means its inevitable disappearance. It is unfortunate that it should too often appear as a dumping ground for party wheelhorses. This is not to say that partisan appointments must be outlawed: there are capable and competent people dedicated to the advancement of ideas portrayed by one or other of the political parties. M. J. Coldwell would have been an asset to the Senate, but although approached many times he always turned it down. There is no reason why a government in power should not appoint people from other parties, and not only from the official Opposition but from the N.D.P. and Social Credit as well. Such appointments have resulted in acquisitions of the calibre of Ernest Manning, Eugene Forsey, and more latterly Ike Smith, former Conservative Premier of Nova Scotia. Former Prime Ministers should automatically be offered Senate posts; in recent years this would have given the Upper House men like St. Laurent, Diefenbaker, and Pearson, if they had chosen to serve.

The Senate and the House of Commons together make up Parliament, something that is often forgotten. I would have enjoyed being a member of the House of Commons because of the opportunity to take part in resolving national issues. I'm not ashamed of being a party man for over sixty years. It's the party system that makes the wheels go round. Putting it in simple terms, if you want to be a football player, you have to play on a team. An independent in the House of Commons is like a wall-flower at a dance. Caucus is where you make your mark, and independents don't get to caucus.

What Parliament is all about is freedom. I said in a Senate speech in December 1968:

> Everybody now is for speed. There is a sort of speed mania; and every
> night on television we hear so-called constitutional authorities
> mouthing and repeating clichés about bringing Parliament into the

twentieth century. You might as well say we should bring freedom into the twentieth century because freedom is all that Parliament is about. Parliament is not a legislative mill. Parliament is not a production line turning out statutes as General Motors turns out motor cars. Parliament, basically, is a place of accountability, a place to check the Queen's estimates and hold the executive to account.

For sixty years I have been observing the resistless drift from Liberalism as Laurier knew it, as Lapointe knew it, as Cardin knew it, as King and St. Laurent knew it. A drift from freedom. We have been turning the government over to the young men in the grey flannel suits.

I think I have made it plain that I am not a professional libertarian; I don't go around shouting about absolute freedom. I do not feel that I have any right to impose my views on my fellow man.

I have consistently advocated expert, professional research facilities for the Opposition, to place them on a par at least with government ministers who have the expertise of large departments at their finger-tips.

On the other hand, if the Opposition made better use of the research facilities at their disposal — the Parliamentary Library and its Research Branch, the caucus research groups — a great change would come over the face of Parliament. Many M.P.'s, and Senators for that matter, feel that if they have read the morning *Globe and Mail* they have accomplished their research for the day.

What is required to make the Opposition work is for the parties sitting opposite the Treasury benches to disabuse themselves once and for all of the iniquitous notion that they are in some way a kind of annex of government, and to return to the blood-and-iron philosophy of simpler days when Oppositions knew where their duty lay. It was to harass and criticize and dragoon and finally destroy the government. It would be attributing too much to human nature to assume that a government in power since 1968 does not have in its closet a formidable collection of skeletons. And yet, looking at the House in recent years one would be inclined to believe that everything was at its best in a perfect world where a complacent Opposition, big with salary increases and large pensions, gazed benevolently across at an equally self-satisfied government, swollen with power and privilege.

This is the crux of the issue. The people — voters, taxpayers — are entitled to be represented not only by a government but by an Opposition which probes, thunders, criticizes, holds up to the light every activity of government. Rising prices, the plight of the farmer and the consumer, the curious "togetherness" of government and industry, the incredible stoppages in essential government services already paid for by the taxpayers, and the incredible arrogance of the leaders of public-service "unions", whose security and economic well-being arise from a contract not with a private employer but with the people of Canada: these are the issues which would have roused a Meighen, a Bennett, a Drew to hammer-and-tongs onslaughts on the Treasury benches instead of apathetic acquiescence.

I have never been an enthusiastic admirer of Speeches from the Throne. I have referred to them in editorials and speeches as pallid exercises in tedium; faint, feeble, flickering reflections; promissory notes of a government on its way to political bankruptcy. In September 1968 I dwelt in this wise on the Speech from the Throne laboriously brought forth by the new Trudeau government.

Some objection was taken recently in the other place to the fact that the Speech from the Throne did not mention the name of Her Majesty.

... Honourable Senators, I submit to you this was not the chief grievance of the Queen. Her chief grievance was this anemic English, this collection of platitudes in the mouth of her representative.

... It is an apologia for doing nothing. It is an impertinence; more than that, a political pamphlet.

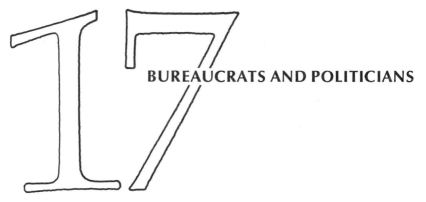

BUREAUCRATS AND POLITICIANS

I have sometimes spoken in harsh terms of the bureaucracy. When it was my job as an editor to send young men up to cover Parliament in the Press Gallery, I said something like this: "Don't worry about press releases and press conferences. They are not news. The news is not what they want you to know but what they don't want you to know. Get out and dig. Talk to people. Get the facts. Don't waste your time re-writing government handouts."

I think it is still good advice. The bureaucracy now is bigger, better organized, with literally hundreds of ex-newsmen in the ranks, their job to extol the performance of some minister or deputy-minister. Fortunately there are still hard-headed people in the communications business who know that their job is not to defend government but to get facts.

Important decisions are made by bureaucrats. This would be bad enough; but it is now almost impossible to find out on what basis decisions are being made; how much they will take out of the pockets of taxpayers; and above all who will benefit. Most disturbing of all, no one seems to care.

Most people get "live" information from television and turn to the press for confirmation and substantiation. Television is under the aegis of the CBC, a government agency which, although individual broadcasters may show courage, is going to be pretty careful not to damage its relations with the Ministry. Other networks, even when privately operated, are under the gun of the C.R.T.C., another all-powerful government agency. They, too, must be careful about "blotting their copybook".

Members of Parliament, whose job is to criticize, question,

analyse, and judge the performance of the government, are in danger of becoming part of the establishment, with salaries, pensions, research staff, paid trips under the aegis of the benevolent and all-wise bureaucracy for which the Cabinet is often merely a front. Cabinet acts on the advice of the bureaucracy; gets its information from the bureaucrats. Very often legislation originates with the bureaucracy and is designed to clear up administrative anomalies or cater to the convenience of those who administer the laws rather than those who are affected by them and must live with them.

Since departmental estimates have been removed from Parliament and relegated to parliamentary committees, the work of scrutiny once done by the entire House is now done by a handful of members. A deputy-minister or a bureau chief comes in, is asked a few perfunctory questions, and departs. We have even had cases where top officials, such as the Clerk of the Privy Council, have been barred by the Prime Minister from giving evidence before a parliamentary committee. The beginning of erosion is the deliberate withholding of information.

In the prevailing climate of "Don't rock the boat" it is unlikely that either M. P.'s or members of the press are prepared to make an issue of Parliament's right to have full information on expenditures. Enormous, mushrooming, self-renewing departments like CIDA (Canadian International Development Agency) are completely outside the ken of Parliament. With its budget of $800 million for expenditure in foreign countries, there is no way of either knowing or controlling, as far as Parliament is concerned, what CIDA is about.

Liberal governments since Mackenzie King have tended to mesh with the bureaucracy to the point at which it has become impossible to tell where government begins and bureaucracy leaves off. Governments have been prolific in spawning task forces and commissions whose function is to second-guess without detracting one iota from the powers of the bureaucracy. Somewhere on the surface of the shapeless mass, like tiny astronauts on a moon landscape, elected governments grope their puny and ineffectual way. M. P.'s and ministers come and go; public servants go on forever, through security of tenure assuming the role of policy makers, and in time policy masters.

On many occasions I have given my views on the Canadian Broadcasting Corporation, a gigantic monolith feeding at the public trough in the name of Canadian culture, a preponderance of second-rate American fare with a few make-weight Canadian talk shows thrown in. I have pointed out many times the CBC's lack of responsibility to Parliament and the taxpayers. Obsessed with the psychology of spending, the CBC is a state within a state, an entity above criticism, a bureaucratic untouchable.

Air Canada is another bureaucratic extravaganza which appears to be completely out of control. The revelation by a top executive that he had the power to sign a cheque of over $100,000 with no questions asked is one of the strangest statements to come out of the bureaucratic never-never land in a long time.

Another thing that has changed is the accessibility of leaders. It is difficult to communicate with a man riding around in a bullet-proof Cadillac. As a reporter I was always able to see the Prime Minister, provided I had a good reason. And, generally, I didn't ask unless I had a good reason. Not long ago, I had occasion to see Mr. Trudeau on a question involving our relations with the United States. I called the Prime Minister's Office and was told to come at five o'clock. He was closeted with a group of diplomats and I had to wait a few moments until he came out, muttering apologies. I gave him my views, from the shoulder.

"What you are telling me," he said, "is directly opposite to the information I have from my officials."

"Then," I said, "your officials are mistaken." I explained my position in detail; he promised to check into the matter, and did.

The incumbent in the position of Prime Minister in our system holds awesome power. A nod, a gesture, is sometimes enough to bring about results from the horde of assistants and second-guessers who now wheel and dip around the throne. It was not ever thus; but in recent years we have taken steps to eliminate some of the checks and balances infused by Britain's genius for parliamentary organization. Since the King-Byng crisis the Governor General has been shorn of real power. The Office of the Privy Council is now but an adjunct to the Prime Minister's Office;

the Senate is rapidly being reduced to a kind of elephants' graveyard for superannuated politicians; and even the Commons has failed to maintain its prestige.

I have had a ringside seat at the game of Ottawa politics for something like sixty-five years. I have watched prime ministers from Laurier to Trudeau. They all had one thing in common: they preferred to tolerate the inconveniences of the position rather than take steps to leave it voluntarily.

In recent years I have been impressed and dismayed by the irresistible growth of bureaucratic power and bureaucratic privilege. The offices of the deputy-ministers in the Ottawa establishment give the show away. They have all the opulence of those of Hollywood producers in the golden era of film. Ministers' offices pale into Spartan insignificance by comparison with the high-rise eyries, carpeted and draped like plush cocktail lounges, in which the appointed servants of the people hold sway.

One deputy-minister until recently entertained visitors in a downtown office recreating French Colonial style, even to the costly pegged Breton floorboards and authentic Quebec pine cabinets. Another, perched in a tower overlooking the Ottawa, was able to look down with heady superiority on the elected representatives toiling in the muggy tawdriness of the Centre Block.

The real government of Canada is carried on from the Office of the Prime Minister and the Office of the Privy Council. This means that a dozen top bureaucrats who advise the Prime Minister, who draw up Cabinet presentations, and who sit in on top-level strategy, are in a position to upstage Parliament, at least in the day-to-day unfolding of management strategy.

The President of the CBC, the Governor of the Bank of Canada, and the President of the Canada Development Corporation wield power unheard of in Laurier's day. Many years ago Clifford Sifton, whose greatness is in danger of being forgotten, said the most worth-while function the Senate could perform was to defend the citizens against the crushing power of the bureaucracy. It is now almost too late; such is the power of the bureaucracy that Parliament has little leverage against it.

The Prime Minister is surrounded by advisers who not only put legislation together, but also create it, generally in terms of the political advantage of the party in power. As I said in the Senate on September 30, 1969:

> Certainly the House of Commons does not know what is going on; nor do we know. Legislation is sent over to us and we examine it as best we can but we do not know upon whose advice that legislation is drafted.

The evolution of power is epitomized in the growing chasm between the Prime Minister and ordinary Canadians. How many Canadians are driven about in an eighty-thousand-dollar automobile, or sport about in a two-hundred-thousand-dollar pool? Symbols of the growing distance separating the holder of the the office from the rest of us. It was not always this way.

There are people still alive who remember Sir Wilfrid Laurier taking the streetcar from his home on Laurier Avenue (Maria Street) to the House of Commons. Louis St. Laurent used to walk down Elgin Street to the Roxborough. I suppose it was a simpler and more stable era. Who, after all, would have wanted to assassinate the Prime Minister of Canada in Laurier's day?

It is a world from which Laurier and Borden would have turned away with a shudder of disbelief. At ease amid culture and decency, they would have been ill at ease in an era of aircraft hijacking and the slaughter of innocent people by crazed fanatics, in the name of "liberation".

Speaking of culture, it is true that our Prime Ministers have not generally been cast in the literary tradition of the Prime Ministers of Britain. Disraeli was a successful novelist, Asquith and Curzon were acceptable writers, Churchill was one of the outstanding stylists of the age. With but few exceptions our Prime Ministers have not been noted for a literary turn of mind. Macdonald, it is true, had a well-stocked library. One of my proud possessions is a book from that library in which, underlined by Macdonald, is an address by the great Irish lawyer John Philip Curran. Macdonald's library contained the best contemporary novelists and volumes of British and Irish oratory. However, it is only rarely that you come across literary allusions in Sir John A.'s speeches.

Laurier was something different. He made himself familiar with history and biography; he could quote Mazzini, Cavour, Garibaldi, with whose aspirations for a united Italy he sympathized. The names of the great British Liberals, Fox, Bright, Gladstone, and O'Connell, were familiar to his lips.

Arthur Meighen's speeches are liberally sprinkled with quotations ranging from Macaulay to Shakespeare. Meighen was particularly fond of Shakespeare; there is a speech of his on record in which he extemporaneously explored the grandeur of Shakespeare's genius with the taste and skill of a Coleridge or a Swift. Meighen's legacy of erudition and enlightenment lingers in his speeches, unsurpassed as when they were delivered.

Mackenzie King's social-science potboiler, *Industry and Humanity*, hardly qualifies him for a place in either literature or politics. Bennett was a great reader — of stockbroker's reports. Diefenbaker, an omnivorous reader of biographies, quoted widely from political figures of another era. Pearson, more academically inclined, had a nodding acquaintance with McLuhan and Galbraith and was not above reading *Fanny Hill*.

Trudeau, the most intellectual of our Prime Ministers, has shown familiarity with Lord Acton. His intellectualism, narrow, academic, is rather cold and theoretical. A number of people were surprised when he admitted he hadn't read Aleksander Solzhenitsyn.

When it came to oratory there was no surpassing Laurier. You may search the masterpieces of British eloquence without finding anything to touch Laurier's speech on Riel. His speech on Regulation 17 which forbade teaching in French in Ontario schools was in the same category.

I cannot speak of Laurier without saying something of Edward Blake, a giant of modern Liberalism, perhaps more than Laurier the father of the modern Liberal Party. Most young Liberals today are unaware of the stature Blake enjoyed as a party philosopher and an exponent of modern political themes. It is a political tragedy that Blake, who preceded Laurier as leader of his party, should be almost forgotten. Blake refused the chief-justiceship of Canada at forty-two. After resigning as leader he went to Ireland and fought for Home Rule. He became a member of the British

House, where it was said only Gladstone himself could rival Blake's power. It was Blake who was selected to act as counsel in the inquiry held into the famous Jameson Raid into the Transvaal which foreshadowed the Boer War. Edward Blake, like R. B. Bennett, is a victim of history, an object of popular neglect; probably for the same reason that Bennett is neglected, the sneaking belief that by going to England they had "left the ship". Canada is jealous of her heroes.

I had great admiration for Sir Robert Borden. He represented something essentially Canadian, a hard-grained stick-to-it-iveness that won the respect of all who knew him. He was not a man to trifle with. Few reporters in the Parliamentary Press Gallery of the day would have dared throw the kind of questions at him that are now considered normal fare for Prime Ministers. One look from Borden would quell the stoutest heart. But in spite of his hard-rock exterior, Borden was capable of delicate flights of fancy. Read his *Letters to Limbo*. Here was the essence of the man, poet and dreamer encased in the hard-shell Halifax lawyer: reflections on the sun setting over the West Block which enter the realm of literature.

In all the years I spent observing and participating in public life, the outstanding intelligence to grace the halls of Parliament was Arthur Meighen. His powerful attacks on the welfare state, on the growing power of bureaucracy, on the destruction of the human spirit by overwhelming government paternalism, have been borne out one hundred per cent. Attending the Imperial Conference in 1921 as Prime Minister, Meighen found time to visit Liberalism's elder statesman, Lord Morley, the biographer of Gladstone and the author of *On Compromise*, perhaps the greatest work of modern times on the art of politics; and they chatted as intellectual equals. Morley, who was capable of writing a sentence like: "It has often been said that he who begins life by stifling his convictions is in a fair way for ending it without any convictions to stifle", found in Meighen an interlocutor capable of understanding his meaning. When they met, two years before the death of the philosopher of British Liberalism, it was one of the experiences of Arthur Meighen's life.

I had considerable respect for T. A. Crerar, who left Borden's

Union Government to head the Progressive Party because he felt the West was getting a bad deal from Ottawa. Although his party had more seats than the Conservatives in 1921, he declined to sit as Leader of the Opposition and in subsequent elections watched his party become absorbed by Mr. King. Finally, Crerar himself joined King's Cabinet, where he served until he went to the Senate in 1945.

At his death in 1975, I spoke these words:

> I knew him in those far years when he was a member of the Union Government serving this country with devotion and distinction. I watched him put off his armour and then like Cincinnatus return to his fields; and then I saw him come back again, come out of the West, beckoning us all to the uplands where, as he put it lyrically, the air was pure and sweet. Then a bit more sadly, I saw him join a Liberal ministry, standing there like Ruth amid the alien corn. In later years I followed his career in the Senate, giving it the rich wisdom garnered from long years, almost the lone survivor of a breed now all but extinct, the breed of Liberals who used to know what Liberalism was about.

Another of the "extinct" breed, Charles Gavan Power bore through life the nickname "Chubby", an indication of the high and affectionate regard in which he was held by political friends and foes alike. Of that curious and anachronistic race, Quebec Irishmen, whose presence is a bright thread in the historical tapestry of the province: the Flynns, O'Neills, Ryans, Lords, Fitzpatricks, Devlins, coming as strangers and waifs of disaster, part of the fibre of the old province.

Chubby Power, with a record of service in two wars, Minister of Defence for Air under Mackenzie King, walked out of the Cabinet, not because he did not believe that conscription must come, but because he could not go back on his word to his constituents.

In September 1968 I said this about him:

> When Senator Power published his book last year, he sent me a complimentary copy and on the flyleaf wrote this:

"To note the remarkable fact that through fifty years of disagreement about almost everything, not an angry word ever passed between us and we Irish and Quebec Irish at that."

I knew him first when he arrived in the House in 1917, fresh from the war, and I followed his career in the various portfolios which, important as they were, were far from a measure of his contribution to his party and the country. From the very first he burst into the House like a "joyous firecracker"; he spoke with wit, pathos, and charm, "sometimes with that cadence of brooding celtic melancholy reminiscent of the great Timothy Healey, for long years a glory at Westminster".

He was a wit, a raconteur, a man who could take a drink with the best of them and remain a gentleman. A loyal supporter of Mackenzie King and his party, his first concern was for the people of his riding. He was not above telling stories on himself. After many years of replying in person to his constituents, he decided they deserved better treatment and hired a young university student, a master of the French language, to handle his correspondence. Meeting some constituents on the streets of Quebec, he found that the eagerly awaited reaction was not quite what he expected. "We don't understand you any more, Mr. Power, since you have begun writing these new kinds of letters." Chubby went back to writing his own letters.

In the Senate he was a monument of good sense and moderation, his practical knowledge cutting to the core of complex problems. Parliament and the country are the poorer for his loss.

In 1967, an Irish Roman Catholic, boasting only the rudiments of formal education, I was named rector of one of Canada's great universities, a seat of Protestant Presbyterian learning. Senator John J. Connolly, distinguished product of another great centre of learning, Notre Dame University at South Bend, Indiana, where something is known of the game of football, raised the matter in the Senate in a kindly and, of course, witty way:

It will not be the first time, honourable Senators, for Scots to welcome the ministrations of their brother Celts, the Irish. St. Columba and his monks went to Iona centuries ago to bring to the pagan Scots the light of Christianity. Senator O'Leary will now bring to the Scots at Queen's his lofty love of language and sense of history. . . .

Well, of course, all this was deeply moving and I replied as humbly as I might, recalling John Morley's well-known saying that even the best man's life was a hard campaign with some lost battles.

Again and again, with life's marching steps, my mind turned back to that village where headstones marked the Irish names, until they were effaced by wind and rain.

"I think," I said in one speech, "of the old village of Gaspé . . .

We never heard of the Government, let alone Government assistance. Yet every person there, their fathers shipped to those rocky shores, wrested a little farm from those stern hills and everything they needed they raised, vegetables from their own garden, milk and meat from their own livestock, produced their own butter and eggs. I sold butter at fifteen cents a pound, eggs at ten cents a dozen.

I went on to speak of the current picture:

What do I find when I return to the same village? Rows and rows of once neat little farms are now ugly with weeds and switch grass, buildings tumbling down, the farms deserted. . . .

Shades of Goldsmith's "Deserted Village"! Instead of stopping decay, government policy encourages it. Generations who have lived in one place are encouraged to move in pursuance of some bureaucratic edict and take their places in the unemployed lines in the cities. Meanwhile, the government moves in and claims the land, "to hastening ills a prey", and soon the major landlord in the country will be the federal government.

FOREIGN AFFAIRS

I have not hesitated over the years to criticize the preoccupation of various Liberal governments — and others — with international problems, sometimes to the neglect of serious domestic difficulties. I often think of Churchill's description of those with "a passion for distant freedoms".; Canadians who get more involved emotionally with what is going on in some obscure corner of some far distant continent than with what is happening under their noses.

A great deal of Canada's inflated posture in foreign affairs can be attributed to Mike Pearson, who rose to prominence in the post-war years as our Minister in charge of External Affairs, and as Prime Minister very often acted as though he continued to occupy his old position. Recently the Rambouillet incident, when France refused to invite Canada to an international economic conference, provided a more realistic measure of our status.

I have often had recourse to a homely sea metaphor in describing our foreign position. We are putting too much sail on the ship. I remember a few years ago speaking to a former Prime Minister at the Rideau Club about some domestic matter. "No one is interested in domestic questions any more. It is all foreign affairs," he told me.

Then there are the internationalists who make a point of knowing the name of every member of the U.N. Security Council but cannot for the life of them remember the members of the Cabinet.

In May 1964, in the Senate, I dealt with the growth of the Department of External Affairs:

I remember when the Department consisted of Sir Joseph Pope and one stenographer. Sir Wilfrid Laurier had a man named William Mackenzie who kept him informed by clipping the foreign press, mainly the London Times. I remember when the Department was under Loring Christie with a staff of four or five. Later it was under Dr. Skelton with a small staff.

I find little excuse for the world-wide vagabondage of minor government officials on self-assigned missions to the far corners of the globe.

My memories of the Commonwealth go back a long way. It was a different organization when Meighen represented Canada in London in 1921. It took courage to stand up to Britain and point out the folly of British policy internationally. He stood against the great minds of Empire — Lloyd George, Curzon, Birkenhead. He had with him one adviser from External Affairs, Mr. Loring Christie. Contrast this with the endless streams of officials who attend the most minor gathering dealing with the most obscure questions of the day.

The original memorandum proposing a Canadian Minister to Washington was drawn up by Loring Christie. It has been retained in my possession over many years. These are the things that do not appear in the history textbooks.

I cannot forbear mentioning the Potsdam Conference of 1946, Harry Truman's first appearance at a gathering of world importance. The conference made a joke of Woodrow Wilson's "open covenants openly arrived at". Five hundred reporters never got any closer than fifteen miles. A former Hearst man, a brigadier-general, was in charge of briefings. He said Truman had charmed Stalin by playing the "Missouri Waltz". Stalin had donned a white coat for the occasion. We managed to absorb these earth-shaking revelations unmoved.

I have taken part in meetings of international parliamentary associations, including the NATO Parliamentary Association and others, and I have been concerned at the way in which Canada selects her representatives to these gatherings.

In 1965 I was asked to be a delegate to the NATO Parliamentary Association in New York. Parliament had been dissolved. M.P.'s were involved with the general election. Two or three days before the conference opened, I was asked to go along. In the British delegation were people of the calibre of Sir Gladwyn Jebb, formerly British Minister to the United Nations and a former Ambassador to France, the author of an authoritative book on foreign affairs. With him was Baroness Elliott, a leading light in the British Conservative Party.

The Americans included Senator Leverett Saltonstall, that Lincolnesque figure from Massachusetts; Senator Clifford Case of New Jersey, one of the ablest members of the U.S. Senate; Senator Jacob Javits from New York; and Senator Robert Kennedy. Dean Rusk, the Secretary of State, was also present on behalf of the Americans. The other delegations were of equally high calibre. Chubby Power had come down with us but was unfortunately called away in the middle of the conference. This left Senator Lionel Choquette, an able and charming personality, and myself to uphold this country. We felt out-classed, out-gunned, and out-generalled.

A resolution came forward referring to the integration of American and European forces in NATO, with never a word about Canada's substantial contribution. It was taken for granted we were included as part of the American contribution. I got that changed by raising a little hell. Is it any wonder many Canadians feel it is time for a long look at NATO and an answer to the question, just what are we doing on the continent of Europe, presumably for the protection of France and Germany, whose forces are many times the size of ours?

I complained about sending troops to Cyprus. Why should Canadians rush in as a human bulwark so Greeks and Turks shall not kill one another? What has this misplaced altruism got to do with Canada or any area of Canadian policy? Even more important, what has it got to do with the Canadian taxpayer? We are not a great or even a middle power, and if others don't see fit to shoulder the burdens of international responsibility why should Canadians spend great sums in pursuit of an inflated, ego-serving ideal?

As for the United Nations organization itself, it has reached a new low in prestige. The suggestion that in order to meet our U.N.

commitments Canadians must sit down with terrorist groups whose purpose is to blow up women and children, set off bombs in crowded streets, shoot up schools with automatic fire, is sufficient measure of the moral disarray in which the United Nations now finds itself. When the United Nations made terrorism respectable, it destroyed its own authority.

The League of Nations was wrecked by its refusal to take a stand on Mussolini's invasion of Ethiopia. The U.N. is now in a position in which a handful of nations from the Third World, backed by the Soviet Union, are calling the tune in favour of violence, guerrilla tactics, murder, and sudden death. You cannot build world peace on organized anarchy.

I must say something about Ireland. I have found occasion to visit the beloved land many times in my lifetime. I have often stayed at a little inn at Adair, during the war full of R.A.F. officers in mufti. There is an old castle there and an old church and a bar and winding Irish roads and Irish faces and Irish speech, and it is like coming home.

I was raised in the bosom of the Irish movements, even though a wide sea away; Emmet, Wolfe Tone, Parnell, Redmond were heroes in a pantheon of exile. When I learned that De Valera was dead, my mind went back to the hawklike face as I saw it in Dublin in the war; and the gaunt, dark, stiff figure sentenced by the British to hang. They said he was a gunman. He was more than that. He was an Irish gentleman, a man of learning and culture, who fought for the land of his mother as he would have fought for his mother herself.

The land which gave to us Yeats and Colum and Shaw, Sean O'Faolain and O'Flaherty, Joyce and Frank O'Connor; which was tortured and torn by fanatics and demagogues, bigots and extremists on both sides: one of the dearest wishes of my heart is to see her united, North and South, a member once again of the Commonwealth of Nations, remembering the words of Henry Grattan, "The Irish Sea cries out against Union; but the Atlantic thunders against separation."

Her children have been swept away to the four corners of the earth, their genius and pride rising again on a soil that was not their own: in letters the imagery and pathos of Eugene O'Neill, in politics the uniqueness of the Kennedys; Irish names sprouting like exotic blooms in far lands: in Chile, O'Higgins, in France, MacMahon, names to be reckoned with in the honour rolls of empires.

Disraeli with his usual prescience said the only workable policy with regard to Ireland was to see to it that the Irish should be able to obtain without violence everything they thought they might hope to obtain by violence. Not bad advice in dealing with a race where love of freedom is a disease to be cured only by freedom itself.

The Irish in America and Canada, often unlettered victims of a school system placing creed above learning, have contributed their tradition of eloquence. The House has been enthralled by the words of a McGee or a D'Alton McCarthy or a Charles Murphy or a C. G. Power — what John Morley once called "the glory of words". There was nothing small about them, nothing of the littleness of petty nationalism which seeks justification for failure in hatred of others.

In far too many ways the attitudes and postures of "Little Canadians" motivated by grudging hatred of everything American are reminiscent of Quebec extremist groups, their hatred directed at everything coming from English Canada.

I said in the Senate on October 14, 1969:

There are people in this country, unfortunately, who are still fighting the Battle of Lundy's Lane. There are some academics who are allowed on "Viewpoint" on the CBC and given $75.00 as well, and on any night at all, they will tell you how we are in peril of being engulfed by the American monolith, how we are affected by American materialism and how in due course, the barbarians are going to pitch their tents among us.

In a fairly long life I have had the privilege of speaking to American audiences in every state of the Union from Maine to California. I have been Ottawa correspondent for American newspapers. I have written for American periodicals. I have been on six Canada—U.S. delegations. I can say truthfully that I never once met an American of consequence who wanted to interfere with Canada's future.

In March 1970 I spoke at Houston, Texas, to a meeting of the Canada—United States Interparliamentary Group. In that speech I attempted to bring out some fundamental principles underlying the relationship between the two countries, so close and yet in many ways so widely separated. My speech was received with good will and attention by the Americans present.

The people of Canada like the people of the United States are basically North Americans, inheritors of the thought and traditions of Europe but also the children of geography, products of the environment, the emotions, the driving forces, the faith, the dreams and the forms of expression of this North American content. Yet there is a difference, a difference I plead with you not to forget. For while Canada and the United States may have the same basic cultures, they each at the same time have domestic and other tasks and problems, political, social and economic which differ widely.

Canada's particular responsibilities, her government, her constitutional structure, her ideals and aspirations, her memories and milestones, even her discords, are facts in her existence which cannot easily be approached understandingly or usefully by another country even though that country be as friendly as yours. Only Canadians can know and resolve such things and we are determined to resolve them in our own way, in the indispensable way of a sovereign society. A bit of this continent from earth to sky we want to call our very own. Wanting that, resolving to have it, we need not be enemies but will pray always that as God has made us neighbours justice will make us friends.

Measured by human history, yours is a young country. Yet standing at the cock crow and the morning star you are at a pinnacle of power, with an awesome accountability to history. If in the discharge of that responsibility you seek peace with justice then we as an ally and friend but never as a satellite, will walk with you always.

For if peace be but a pause to identify the next enemy, if our world be unable to find a moral equivalent for the hydrogen bomb, then despair will have the last word, Death's pale flag will again be advanced and this planet may well cease to be the abode of men.

The speech was read in its entirety into the Congressional Record by Senator Frank Church of Idaho. It was a theme I had many times touched on, the unwritten and yet honoured pledges, sealed by history, between Canada and the United States.

In April 1970, speaking in the Senate, I dealt with the United States in these terms:

> I make no apology for saying, Thank God for the United States. Some of my friends have said at one time I wanted to bar American magazines from Canada. Nothing could be farther from the truth. The Royal Commission of which I was Chairman made no such recommendation or anything remotely like it. Again and again we rejected any attempt to inject anti-Americanism into the commission's findings.

I suppose anti-American bias has been a feature of Canadian political life at least since 1775 when the Americans invaded Canada and were driven back at Quebec by Guy Carleton. In the reciprocity election of 1911, candidates against Laurier appeared on platforms wearing Union Jacks for vests, a kind of anti-Americanism rampant then—now, I hope, dead forever.

We share with the Americans a common continental culture. Mark Twain and James Fenimore Cooper are part of that heritage and so are Charles G. D. Roberts, Stephen Leacock, Ralph Connor, and Lucy Maud Montgomery. We share the splendid literary heritage of the English-speaking world, Shakespeare, Dickens, Thackeray, Fielding, Swift, Pope, Addison, Defoe. These things we own in common.

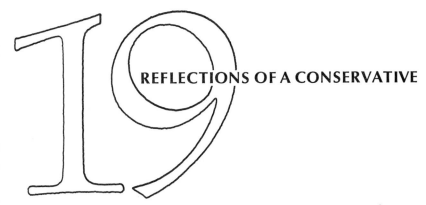

REFLECTIONS OF A CONSERVATIVE

Conservative principles, carried down from the origins of party government when Tory squires held to the twin lodestones of Monarchy and Trade, are no respecters of parties. Believers in the individual's sacred right to run his own affairs hold forth in all parties. Opposed to government getting into business, doing in its heavy-footed way what private capital and private know-how are best equipped to do; opposed to uncontrollable corporations with virtually unlimited funds and obscure purposes backed by the power and authority of the state in the manner of Louis xiv or Charles ii; although they do not refer to themselves as conservatives, they may be described as "latent conservatives".

Conservative leaders from Macdonald to Stanfield were closely joined in respect for individual rights and suspicion of bureaucracy. Where there is a contest or confrontation between individual rights and the rights of the state, you will find Conservatives ranged on the side of the individual.

We live in a society in which it has become conventional wisdom to downgrade politicians. Professional politicians brought into being freedom, built Confederation, preserved for us all the rights won by our fathers. I think of Henri Bourassa and his unending fight to preserve the identity of French Canada: those who benefit today from his efforts scarcely bother to recall his name. I remember his square, blocky figure rising in the House, the utter stillness that preceded his words like the silence that falls before a storm. A storm of eloquence it was, gripping the hearts of all who listened, poured forth with a passion even Laurier could not match.

It cannot be forgotten that it was the Conservative Party under Macdonald and Cartier and Tupper and Tilley and McGee that brought about unity in this nation. We, too, have our history and the grandeur of our past.

The hanging of poor, half-mad Riel drove Quebec into the arms of the Liberal Party, and Laurier's leadership consummated the relationship, the offspring of which was a lease on power interrupted only fitfully by Conservative incursions. On the sidelines of power over too many years the Conservatives developed an opposition mentality, a maverick approach to problems. Even in the seats of the mighty, the Conservatives have all too frequently had the appearance of a party in opposition, flailing away in a sort of behaviouristic reflex.

You cannot have a party wandering down the corridors of time crying out hollowly for absent glories. Macdonald is greatness unchallenged, but the irony is that Macdonald couldn't have built Confederation without Brown; he knew it and Brown knew it.

Macdonald had a wry appreciation of Brown —queer, crabbed, covenanting Brown. Sir Joseph Pope gives us a picture of Brown and Macdonald in Piccadilly with Russell, the great correspondent of *The Times*, all three slightly tiddly after a day at Ascot, blowing peas out of three-penny pea-shooters at passengers in passing buses (horse-drawn, of course). It shouldn't be forgotten that in pushing Confederation Macdonald had everything to gain; but Brown had everything to lose — party, policy, and "Clear Grit" principles. Confederation was the light beckoning at the end of the dark tunnel of deadlock. A great editor brought down by an assassin's bullet, Brown never received the credit he deserved. Forgotten by his party, it is Conservatives who, with affection and appreciation, cherish his memory.

Edmund Burke gave to party what belonged to mankind — heart, mind, and spirit. Without the work of Pitt, Fox, Canning, Disraeli, Gladstone, what would be the human condition? The outlawing of child labour, universal education, universal suffrage is among their monuments.

From Lincoln through Taft and Theodore Roosevelt and Eisenhower (and, yes, Richard Nixon) there is a clear line of American conservative thought. Tragic it is that Republicanism should have been saddled with the incubus of Watergate, which, in destroying a president, narrowly missed destroying the presidency. No one party has a monopoly of scandal; nor for that matter has any one profession.

Americans cherish the memory of their political figures — Washington, Jefferson, Clay, Calhoun, Webster, Lincoln, the Roosevelts, and the Kennedys — while Canadians neglect or ignore theirs. "Politics," Winston Churchill said, "is not a game. It is an earnest business. Party Government is an outstanding feature of the political systems of all branches of the English-speaking world. I know of no equal force which ensures the stability of democratic institutions." Those who would crush out freedom, the capacity to resist tyranny, first crush out the Opposition.

In the election of 1949, when P. D. Ross was at death's door, I received a summons to go and see him. "I suppose," he said in a weak voice, "the party needs money."

"Parties always need money, P.D." He got out his cheque-book and, though he didn't have that kind of money to hand out, he made out a cheque for $10,000 to the National Conservative Party. He died four days later, respected from coast to coast. A clear case of a man contributing without hope of favours in return.

Another time, when P.D. was running for Mayor of Ottawa, a cheque for $1,000 arrived in the mail from Charles Murphy, the most militant of all Liberals. What favours could Charles Murphy expect? Too many people don't understand these things.

Once when we were organizing a national convention of the Conservative Party, I was chairman of the committee raising the money and was approached by one of the more prominent Liberals in Ottawa, who insisted on contributing $5,000 for no better reason than that he believed in the two-party system.

Over the years it has not been a case of "my party, right or wrong": when I have felt my party was wrong, I have not hesitated to say so—too often, perhaps, for the liking of some in the Conservative Party. A political party is not judged by momentary stands, spasmodic positionings, but rather on the record of doctrine and principle accumulated over the years. I value Conser-

191

vatism for its healthy pragmatism, support of individual initiative, the incentive society rather than the ultimate naivete that men will work to achieve abstract ends.

In October 1970, I had some things to say about Conservatism, not only as a political party, but as a moulding force, an instinct for preserving and treasuring what is best and supplying us with tools for survival in a world without beacons. I wrote:

> Before bowing to this bleakness, before kneeling for the final annihilation and leaving God and religion to the theologians I would like a word of dissent about Conservatism, an editing of the wry charity of its obituaries.

A Conservative, I said, was one who believed that "the present has a right to govern itself according to its needs", and it is "as well to create good new precedents as to honour old ones". A Conservative was a person "with a care for prudent advance"; Conservatism itself "an assignment for our survival". The Conservative must be a sceptic, wary of slogans and "political wonder drugs", but always holding a "humanized view" of events. I put the argument in the form of a question: "Whence in our anxious day the irrelevance of Conservatism—the wrong of taking counsel from both times, from the ancient what is best, from the present what is fittest?"

Then I put the issue between the parties as follows:

> In the summary, Conservatism today, rational, humanistic Conservative thought, has nothing to do with hard, implacable, unyielding dogmatism, it is beholden to neither big business, super patriots, nor to technological materialism; but is actually a form of dissent, skeptical of Liberalism with one foot planted firmly in the clouds and asking itself what are the tolerable limits of the state's activity. . . .
>
> Too few of this generation . . . who sneer at Conservatives as Tories . . . realize that it was a leader of the Conservative Party who laid the foundation of the Statute of Westminster; who won separate Canadian representation at the Versailles Peace Conference; who first objected to a British Government nomination of a Governor General for

Canada; first proposed a Canadian as Canada's Governor General and first demanded a Canadian Minister in Washington.

I concluded:

> If in such circumstances Conservatism has ceased to be relevant, its philosophy useless in a vexed, sick society, then hope for the time being bids us farewell.

The Liberal Party, on the other hand, began in Canada as a reform party, a party of popular rights against the Tory squires who surrounded the Governor in Council. Its mouthpieces were Baldwin and Lafontaine and their disciples in the battle for responsible government. But a party in power fifty-four years out of seventy-five cannot be expected to go on reforming with fanatical determination.

The change in the Liberal Party began fifty years ago, brought about by the organizing genius of Charles Murphy and the selection of Mackenzie King as leader, inheriting Laurier's mantle. King's simple formula was to cling at all costs to his Quebec allies; as I wrote in retrospect in 1968:

> ... When business in English speaking Canada saw or thought it saw that King's Conservative opponents could not overcome his sixty or more safe seats in Quebec, it humanly cast its lot with the winner.

Success attracting always fresh support, the Liberal Party became the party of competence, of managerial skill, of people with a talent for governing. Meanwhile the Conservatives pursued a fixed determination to hang themselves on a cross of principle, its relevance not always apparent to the public.

The Liberal establishment through its years of power received firm and solid backing from the praetorian guard of the Ottawa bureaucracy, whose approval or disapproval could make or break governments.

Confronted by a Liberal Party which betrays its past, little more than a fortuitous collection of conflicting ingredients held together by desire for power (witness the recent resignation of John Turner as Minister of Finance, perhaps the only idealist in the ranks of the Trudeau government), the ordinary Canadian finds hope in a Conservative Party, though it is frequently plagued by fools and demagogues mixing stupidity with achievement, and is too often the victim of a blind death-wish.

To view with any hope of realism the current state of Canadian politics, it must be recognized that the real struggle is not between parties but between individual rights and the crushing power of bureaucracy.

In spite of programs, policies, and other semantic roundelays dreamed up to mystify electors, politics is essentially a matter of people administering people, something that many experts have been reluctant to grasp.

It is the strength of Conservatism to make known the defects of the system while preserving its effectiveness. And, of course, it is really people who decide whether a system will work by the degree of effort and dedication they put into making it work.

The privilege and pleasure of being part of the history of the Canadian political system for over sixty years has been immortal wine: the hours and moments spent in the presence of great men. If you ask me about their faults, I say that all, even the best, had faults.

One thing they had in common. All tried to do the best for Canada.

A PERSONAL POSTSCRIPT
by I. Norman Smith

In his book as in his life Grattan O'Leary has generously remembered his friends, colleagues, and antagonists. Yet in his enthusiasm for their qualities and in his zest to talk about Canada, he has said relatively little of himself. That was always his way. The modesty of his book screens the verve and warmth of his nature. He was always young. I shall try in this personal Postscript to fill in between the lines, greatly helped by some words of others, and with a few favourites from my treasury of Grattan's thought and laughter. But first, let's watch him at work, sleeves rolled up, cigarette dangling, as I saw him some years ago at the height of his action.

He used the two-fingered hunt-and-peck system on a beleaguered old typewriter he wouldn't give up, and he beat the hell out of it at a terrific clip. When in flight his jockey-like body was hunched over the machine, swaying incessantly backward and forward, his face sometimes swooping almost down to the keyboard. Feverishly he'd read the half-sentences as they came out, his lips working at them so his ear would get the music or spacing of the message. If it didn't "read", he'd cross it out with a vicious tattoo on the "x" and "m" keys, and do the sentence again until it did. If he didn't notice you standing in his door during these birthing moments, it would be partly because of the haze rising from a cigarette into his eyes; partly for the din of the machine; partly because his thoughts were wholly on the cause he was pleading or damning.

He worked in his vest. The cheap wood typewriter table was black with cigarette burns. Suddenly he'd dart into one of our offices to borrow a cigarette or a match, never returning it.

His main desk was a kind of compost heap. A big round pile of stuff, usually twelve or fifteen inches high, filled either side of the surface, so that in front of him was a valley clear of everything except the clips or notes he was working on.

The two mounds had no separate purpose. There were personal letters and bleats to the editor; there were household bills and old Racing Forms. There were texts of other men's speeches, sent for praise and receiving the grace of storage treatment prior to oblivion. Sometimes one of us would get an appeal from a high or low source asking couldn't he get an answer to the question he had ages ago written to O'Leary. With optimism born of experience, I'd go in and he'd say: "Oh God, didn't I answer that—here, I know where it is." With that, his hand would not touch either mound but sort of hover over it; and then he would insert thumb and forefinger into the slope and extract it. "You answer it, will you Norman; he's a curious fellow, really, but a dear soul and we should answer him."

Forgetful, yes, but charmingly so. Not infrequently he'd lose his glasses, and call out for an office-boy, give him fifty cents, and tell him to go to Woolworth's "and buy what they call their reading glasses in black frames, they're in a tray on the right side."

The man who never returned a cigarette was the easiest touch in the office for a loan to any man in the building. I'm sure he lost on that, but he never pressed anyone. The man who'd forget to go and make his speech almost never had to look up quotations from poets or politicians. He'd just bang it down, and it was almost always right. If someone would write, catching him out, he'd say "Run the letter", and thump his fist against his forehead.

In those days he never had much money but his pocketbook always bulged; for he played cribbage or poker almost daily, and kept his winnings in his pocket lest tomorrow he had to pay 'em out. When they raced horses and not buggies at Connaught Park he had still further need for folding cash. He had lost money on most every nag on the continent, but being there with him was a picnic. His back was hunched with hunches: if a jockey's colour was yellow and Grattan had on a yellow tie—that was enough. One day a lady in our group asked him to put five dollars for her on a cripple's nose. Knowing it couldn't run for its life, Grattan didn't place her bet, and of course was going to return her five dollars. It won. He gave her $40 after pretending to cash the ticket. As I had not seen him at the wicket I questioned him, aside. He said, "Now don't you say a word, Norman, I'll win it back next race anyway."

He was more discriminating in picking words, but even so he made writing and editing a game, as others might argue over which fly to use on a dark day or when to use a pitching wedge instead of a nine-iron. Offering a suggestion to him was easy—he seemed delighted that we cared. "Glad you spotted that," he said to me one time. "It's a funny thing about writing, you forget the reader can't know what you have in mind unless you say it." He loved words, loved to weigh them for sound as well as for sense, loved seeking the right one instead of one that would do. Absurd to him would be the idea that a writer should just sit down and let his subconscious roll out to help the great tide of human thought. Grattan believed a newspaper should concern itself with every phase of life, and he used weekends to broaden his vigil. Monday mornings he'd come in, move quickly to his office, and in no time you'd hear the typewriter going: arguing with something in the *New York Times* (which he always read), commenting on a quote in the *New Statesman and Nation,* or venting a printable curse at the travesty that was Friday's prizefight, recalling the great days of fights as though he had spent his life in arenas and poolrooms. There was only one challenge in journalism he knew nothing about—the problem of finding something to write about each day.

I want to say something, too, of the "attitude to work" he showed us all. When the New York *Herald Tribune* folded he wrote an article recalling its flair and character, but then discovered we had already used a two-column piece from the AP. "Throw mine out, the AP's got all my facts and did a better job on the old-timers who wrote for the paper." When Frank Underhill died in 1971 I phoned Grattan to see if he would do a personal recollection. He sent it over with a note saying "My pen is rusty" and asking me to chuck it away if it wasn't right. It was a beautiful piece.

One night about midnight when I was leaving, after writing a signed column on a Commons blow-up, Grattan was coming in to do an editorial.

"Did you get your piece done, Norman?"

"Yes, but I'm kind of worried about it."

"Good; if you weren't worried about it, I would be."

After I thought I was "grown up" he handed back an editorial I had submitted, saying sternly but quietly: "Norman, this is too long and too confused, and it mixes frivolity and seriousness in a way that won't do. But what really worries me about it is that you know it has these faults but didn't work them out of it. That's all I'm going to say." And he walked out.*

What fortune to have been with such a man, and fortunately we all knew it — while he was still with us, after he retired, and now. We'd trade stories about him endlessly. Bill Westwick used to recall with a chuckle the night one of the young reporters came up to Grattan in some awe and asked, "How do you learn to write?" "Get a typewriter and a lot of paper and get going," Grattan replied, much to the boy's joy, for he had thought it would be harder. When Grattan died, Bill, superb old sportsman and sports editor, said simply: "He had a high standard himself, which he set for everybody, but he was forgiving and certainly the most remarkable and lovable man I've ever known." Of John Grace, now editorial editor and vice-president, Grattan once said admiringly at an office party, "He's had far more formal education than any *Journal* man I've known but is a human being even so!" Well, John was almost incredulous of Grattan's patience with the views of others. "He *loved* diversity, wanted his colleagues to write what they believed, as long as we were sensible or defensible." Lou Lalonde, long our General Manager and now President and Publisher, with characteristic brevity and insight said of Grattan: "He had a way of making problems seem fun, something to work at, not worry about. What a man he was!" Grattan had also enjoyed for years a specially close association with Jim McCook,

* The foregoing recollections, with slight changes for brevity's sake, are reproduced from *The Journal Men*, by I. Norman Smith.

because of Jim's integrity and Scottish loyalty to the paper, but also because Jim was knowledgeable and keen about politics. They had great sport in disagreement, no less than in agreement. Jim revered his Irish colleague's humour in enduring all our failings "and the example he set in the protection of good English".

Yes, good humour and good English. As Landor said, "Clear writers like fountains do not seem so deep as they are; the turbid look the most profound." I can hear O'Leary bursting out one time: "Electronic journalism? There is no such thing as electronic journalism. Did you ever hear of electronic poetry?" He would groan on hearing yet again the "venerable and sanctified clichés" of the debate about freedom of the press. "The Fourth Estate, for God's sake, is not the whole community. A great constitutional doctrine cannot be degraded into a commercial convenience!" "I don't know what in the name of God has happened to the press," he wrote in 1974. He felt it was "making gods out of columnists and telecommunicators, whatever that is", and he was pretty disgusted at the way the media were inflaming every little community rumpus into a scandal. "I am just as uncomfortable with the new cry about the public's 'right to know'. Of course the public has a right to know, but *when*, and *how*, and *under what circumstances*?" He believed the press should be more concerned about its right to dig than about getting more government handouts. Were reporters forgetting what Dr. Johnson called the passion for curiosity? "The job of the press is to protest, to expose, to oppose. It may sometimes be wrong but it must protest anyway, must let big business, big government, big anything, know that someone can find them out." As for neutral newspapers and their editors and publishers: "I do not want to talk about neutral newspapers, there is too much violence in the world already."

A softer though perhaps deeper lament of his was that so many reporters and editors in recent years seemed to read little, other than newspapers. Charles Lynch spoke interestingly of this on the CBC the day after the Senator died:

What happens to a mind that's that well stocked when the owner of it dies? Where does all that stuff go? Not only did he have the politics of the century, our politics and world politics, in his head, but literature. The most incredible retentive memory for poetry, particularly Irish poetry—Yeats and others—that he could quote by the hour. He retained everything he read and he read assiduously. You wonder how a man of action would find that much time to read, but reading was very much a part of his being. And he was always very scornful of those of us in journalism who didn't read. He'd say, how can you be in this business and not want to stock your mind with everything you can lay your hands on?

Nearly thirty years ago Grattan gave me a copy of an address delivered by the late Dr. W. E. McNeill when he retired as Vice-Principal of Queen's University. Grattan had heavily underscored these lines:

It is not enough merely to be wise in one's own work. The view is too short. The individual must see beyond his immediate task. Literature records the spiritual history of mankind, its joys and sorrows, hopes and fears, aspirations and defeats, the earthy worst, the heavenly best. It shows life whole.

Grattan read from his youth to the last week of his life. Literature was indeed a part of his being. He read in his zest, wonder, curiosity, and respect for life. And throughout his career his knowledge of literature, in all its forms, star-lit his pleadings and encouragement to the people of his own times and country. I think, for instance of how he used—variously and over decades—Sir William Osler as a kind of springboard to awaken the public. The distinguished physician, in an address in 1910 at the University of Edinburgh, had suggested that civilization was in a state of decay —"man has even outdone what appears to be atrocities in nature." O'Leary would lower his voice and ask, "What would Dr. Osler see now?"—and answer:

He would see rampant materialism, democracy more a way of speech than a way of life, terrifying juvenile delinquency, millions seeking tranquility not through prayer or serene courage but from tranquilizers; he would see television's inanities and vulgarities replacing the home library, a sometimes venal press less concerned with its high mission for freedom than with its own material gain and the vital statistics of Hollywood's latest female star; he would find a longing for the unadventured life, young men hoping for state security at sixty; he would find reasonable movements for legitimate ends degraded by violence and bad manners, by a nauseous racialism parading as patriotism.

Some of us who are a trifle uneasy in the presence of oratory might feel Grattan was having a ball there, so to speak. In a way, yes; but he meant every word of it, passionately, almost religiously. Grattan O'Leary did feel that way, much more often than his cheerful and buoyant presence led people to think. Look at the sculpture of him (1948) in the corridor of Parliament just outside the Reading Room — scowling. Note the expression of heavy concern in the drawing of him by Irma Coucill (1972). A like anxiety is in a portrait of him (1959) by Robert Hyndman, a sensitive Ottawa artist who knew him pretty well, and in the Canadian Press photograph of him at his desk in the Senate (1974). What the artists and camera saw was a principal source of his wisdom and humanity.

Yet new every morning returned the love of life; another chance to draw to a straight, to have a row with the Senate ("a kind of graveyard for elephants"), or yet another reminder of Sir Edward Grey's finding that "the people isn't a great statesman". For variety he would take a shy at the bureaucrats: "This is a simple Bill, but whoever wrote it strove with might and main to make it as complicated as the Einstein theory. When I see bills written as this is written, it almost makes me revert to belief in capital punishment!"

Some people—including Liberals—thought O'Leary was too aggressive, in journalism and politics. Sometimes perhaps he was; but attack was his way of finding out what others thought, or if they thought at all, and what he himself thought. Simulated anger was his favourite shillelagh. I remember once suggesting that a piece he had just typed was overstated. He chortled: "Of course it is; partly because I don't understand it; if I don't overstate it the buggers won't understand it." He was a man not of conviction but of a mass of convictions. He had no awe of consistency. The Toronto *Telegram*, I think it was, once quoted him against himself at an earlier date. He showed it to me with a big grin and exclaimed: "God preserve me from a man who keeps files." He punched out an editorial saying that, but hinting that there might be something to be said for a man who has the wit to change his mind.

For an explosive writer and orator O'Leary was also a good listener; he would look right into your eyes as though x-raying your argument. He believed discussion to be essential to a civilized life, sharing Belloc's view that "it would be the death of controversy to demand a real conquest; when people begin to get into that mood controversy ends and fighting begins." The morning after another Liberal victory O'Leary would come in smiling and do an editorial urging Canadians to give the new government a fair chance. Almost his only abiding rancour was for Big Business and High Society people full of abuse of politicians and politics but too proud to get down into the arena. The bigotry of smugness enraged him: "I have no use for the tolerance of indifference; it is easy to be tolerant if you don't care."

Some have wondered which counted most with O'Leary — politics or journalism. The answer, I think, is both. He loved journalism; praised it, scolded it, and ceaselessly challenged it to do better. When at seventy-four he became a Senator and retired as editor he simply continued his life's interest in politics, giving full time to his burning conviction that the well-being of a people depends on parliamentary democracy. Patrick Watson got him talking about this journalism-politics dualism in a sensitive CBC television interview shortly before he died. Grattan was being critical of the time he had wasted in his life:

> I would have gotten much farther if I had gone—I mean journalism was one thing but politics was the—well—now if Arthur Meighen had won, no question about it, he told me he was going to give me a position in his Cabinet. I would have loved that. I'd love to be in

Parliament. Parliament to me was and is—without Parliament we're nothing.

Watson protested that O'Leary's role in the *Journal* had been important for Canada. "You asked questions that perhaps could not have been asked from within the structure of power. Isn't that a vital role?"

> *O'Leary:* It's a vital role from the standpoint of criticism but it's not a real role. There's something else here too.
> *Watson:* Which is to take the responsibility for a decision and to act?
> *O'Leary:* Right.
> *Watson:* Put your neck on the line?
> *O'Leary:* Right.

And yet, I wonder if Grattan would have gone in with Meighen. I wonder whether P. D. Ross, my father, and friends like Alex Johnston, Grant Dexter, Arthur Ford, T. A. Crerar, and C. G. Power would not have persuaded him that great editors were scarcer than great politicians! It is an interesting question, but the two zeals were one with him anyway. "We must build up a sort of pattern of public thought, a framework of public morality, a realization that democracy's chores are important." That was his life's theme, the source of his caring, of his giving and wanting friendship. Neither life nor politics, he used to say, should be a spectator sport. Politics was a matter of people, and so was journalism. There was nothing in him of that Londoner who, looking out of his club after lunch and seeing that it was pouring, told his friend he wasn't going out but was "just going to sit here by the window and watch the damn people go by". Acquaintances or beloved friends, colleagues, antagonists, taxi-drivers, or porters—he was interested in them all, always had time to be courteous. "His crusty benevolence," said Harry Boyle, "is a national treasure." "He didn't know a single Senate rule," mused his friend John Connolly, former government leader in the Senate, "but he knew better than any of us what the Senate should be about." A waitress at the Rideau Club said: "So poor Senator O'Leary won't be in any more; he was a lovely gentleman. I'll never forget the time I spilled some soup over him. All he did was laugh and then when he saw I was upset he said, 'Oh you poor dear, never you mind at all, just bring me a big wet napkin.'"

In 1973 I asked Grattan what his religion had meant to him. I have reported this elsewhere, but relevant here is the last sentence of his reply:

> I may be dismayed by what has been done by Christians in the name of Christianity, but I balance that by what Christians have done for man's good. In ecumenism I do not believe, I cannot believe in unity of dogma. I do believe in unity of charity. If I believe in the last, and hate cruelty, injustice, intolerance, I am content to face the Unknown.

Father Joseph Birch, of Ottawa's St. Joseph's Church, had long treasured the close friendship and frank arguments he had with Grattan. In his eulogy he said that Grattan was not one of those who "hold the principles of religion at arm's length, as it were, and gaze on them."

Exactly. Grattan knew he was no saint, put on no airs in church or about church, but he made the principles of his religion the goals of his life and work, not forgetting the value of laughter and enchantment. He liked to pass on Chesterton's view that the world would never starve for lack of wonders but that it might well starve for lack of wonder. Grattan often knew anxiety, but it never burdened him. Towards the end of his illness he told Charlotte Gobeil on television that he didn't particularly want to die, but that was up to God to determine. In the meantime he lived through to the end, with extraordinary cheer, keenly watching the passing parade, and grateful that he had been in it. Leaving seemed that simple to him, and was not a battle lost.

INDEX